America's Lost H-Bomb!

Palomares, Spain, 1966

One of 32 nuclear accidents involving U.S. nuclear weapons between 1950 and 1980. — With an "overall look at United States nuclear accidents."

America's Lost H-Bomb!
Palomares, Spain, 1966

by
Randall C. Maydew

Sunflower University Press®
1531 Yuma • P. O. Box 1009 • Manhattan, Kansas 66505-1009 USA

Cover: Courtesy Los Alamos National Laboratory, Los Alamos, New Mexico.

ISBN 0-89745-214-3

Edited by Julie Bush

Layout by Lori L. Daniel

Contents

Acknowledgments

I AM INDEBTED TO Jack Howard for furnishing information on the Pentagon's role during the Palomares search. William R. Barton replaced me as a member of the Systems Analysis Team and contributed valuable technical details. Lori Parrott carefully reviewed this book, as did former Sandia Corporate Historians Mecah Furman and Leland Johnson. Carl Mora, Sandia Corporate Historian, and Myra O'Canna, Corporate Archives, supplied historical information. Tonimarie Stronich Huning provided facts on nuclear safety and was responsible for moving the #4 B28 bomb case from Sandia storage to the National Atomic Museum. Lastly, Larry Moretz, who has a 60-year collection of U.S. Navy books and papers, provided details on Navy ships, systems, and personnel.

Prologue

*I*T WAS Saturday, 22 January 1966.

Alan Pope, Director of Aero Projects at Sandia Corporation, Albuquerque, New Mexico, received an urgent telephone call from the Pentagon. W. J. "Jack" Howard, Assistant to the Secretary of Defense for Atomic Energy, asked Alan if he had seen *Thunderball*, the macho James Bond movie about a missing nuclear bomb.

Alan had, and Jack responded, "Good, because we need your help to locate one that's been missing since the 17th! A B-52G Stratofortress and a KC-135A Stratotanker collided in mid-air over Palomares, Spain."[1]

Jack Howard's other Pentagon job was Chairman of the Military Liaison Committee, the formal channel between the Atomic Energy Commission (AEC) — a civilian-controlled organization set up by Congress in 1947 to manage atomic energy projects — and the Department of Defense (DoD).[2] He was on leave of absence from

Sandia where he was the Director of Systems Development at Sandia's Livermore, California, national laboratory, responsible for nuclear ordnance development. Sandia Corporation, formed in 1945 (now Sandia National Laboratories), was charged with the design of the arming, safing, fusing, and firing systems for a nuclear warhead; the parachute system (jointly with the USAF); and the shape, structure, and aerodynamics of the bomb case.[3] These nuclear ordnance responsibilities supported the Los Alamos warhead designs.

The missing nuclear warhead at Palomares had been designed by the Los Alamos national laboratory.[4] And Jack Howard was knowledgeable about nuclear weapons because for nearly two decades he had both designed and supervised design for Department of Defense weapon systems. He also knew — having worked with Alan Pope at Sandia for some 15 years — that Alan's staff had helped design the complicated parachute system for the missing B28 bomb and could calculate trajectories of descent.

Alan called me at home within a few minutes of the Pentagon call. At the time, I was manager of the Aerodynamics Department at Sandia (1965-1988), responsible for directing a staff of 90 engineers and scientists in the aerodynamic design of nuclear bombs, shells, and missile warheads, as well as parachutes and rockets, for the AEC.[5] Alan and I quickly put together a team to make trajectory calculations, using Sandia's state-of-the-art IBM 7090 computer.

We had already been following the Palomares accident closely since the 20th and knew that three of the bombs carried by the B-52G had been found immediately on the Spanish shore by the Strategic Air Command's 16th Air Force. The 16th, with headquarters at Torrejon Air Force Base near Madrid, was in charge of all SAC operations in Europe.

But the missing fourth nuclear bomb might have fallen into the ocean. Jack asked us to call him back if we thought there was a good probability that it had drifted out to sea.

A quick analysis showed that, indeed, this was a high probability because of the offshore winds. Jack then requested help from Dr. Robert W. Morris, Assistant Secretary of the Navy for Research and Development, and on Sunday, 23 January, Chief of Naval Operations Admiral David L. McDonald established AIRCRAFT SALVOPS MED (Aircraft Salvage Operations Mediterranean), directing mobilization of Navy resources to assist in the search and recovery of the lost nuclear weapon.[6]

At the same time, General Delmar E. Wilson, Commander of the 16th Air Force in Spain, requested that I visit Palomares as a member of a Systems Analysis Team to advise him on where to search for the missing bomb. From 30 January to 11 February I worked with the 16th personnel in the "tent city" erected at Palomares. Of primary concern to us all was that this mid-air collision was the most serious of any of the 28 U.S. nuclear weapons accidents that had previously occurred, with far-reaching national and international implications.[7]

Three of the Palomares bombs had hit the ground, and the high explosives in two of them had detonated at impact, scattering plutonium dust over several hundred acres.

But where was the fourth bomb?

Little did anyone know that it would take 80 days before the elusive weapon was found, at a cost of $50 to $80 million and much adverse international publicity for the U.S. But the missing bomb also resulted in a safer design philosophy regarding nuclear weapons, a philosophy that has continued to benefit the nuclear community and the world to this day.

Chapter 1

The Refueling
Accident

Refueling over Spain . . . had been a standard daily procedure in the CHROME DOME flights since 1961.

C APTAIN CHARLES J. WENDORF was aircraft commander of the B-52G Stratofortress, radio call number Tea 16, from the 51st Bomber Squadron (stationed at Seymour Johnson Air Force Base, Goldsboro, North Carolina), 68th Bombardment Wing of the Strategic Air Command.[8] Captain Wendorf's crew flew special 24-hour CHROME DOME alert missions about every ten days.

OPERATION CHROME DOME was the code name for these Strategic Air Command air-alert missions, in operation since 1961 as a result of the Cold War, in which B-52 Stratrofortresses carried nuclear bombs on four different routes every minute of the day and night. Three of the routes went north, out over Alaska, up above Canada, and out to Greenland to be ready to dip down over the Arctic to bomb Russian targets if needed. The southern route was over the middle Atlantic, across Spain, and up the Mediterranean to near the Soviet-Turkish borders. Our nuclear bombers could fly only over international waters or over friendly territory such as Spain, Greece, and Turkey on this southern route.

The B-52 was the workhorse of this mission — a large, eight-engine, swept-wing aircraft, specifically designed to carry four thermonuclear bombs internally. It served as the primary strategic bomber of the United States Air Force, able to carry a crew of six and to travel approximately 10,000 miles before refueling. The B-52G that Captain Wendorf flew differed slightly from the B-52 in that it had a shorter tail fin for improved stability in high-speed, low-level flight and could carry an air-to-surface missile.

Refueling over Spain, made possible by military agreements signed by the United States and Spain in 1953, had been a standard daily procedure in the CHROME DOME flights since 1961.[9] The main feature of the agreements, renewed and expanded in 1963, called for the use by the United States of a series of air and naval facilities to be operated jointly by Spain. Typical Air Force Strategic Air Command "joint" bases were Torrejon Air Force Base near Madrid and Moron Air Force Base near Seville. The 1953 agreement also gave the United States overflight rights for the nuclear bombers and permission to station SAC attack aircraft and tanker planes on the new bases.

On 16 January 1966, Captain Wendorf and his men took off at dawn from North Carolina on another routine flight, just as they had done dozens of times before. Flying the southern route, they approached the Spanish coast from the northwest after about six hours and were refueled at dusk between Zaragoza and Barcelona from a four-engine KC-135A jet Stratotanker from the joint SAC/Spanish Air Force base at Torrejon. Wendorf and crew then proceeded up the Mediterranean and circled near the Eastern Bloc borders until they were relieved by other SAC aircraft about dawn.

The crew started the nine- to ten-hour flight back to North Carolina, with refueling scheduled over the Almeria coast in southeast Spain on the way home. This second refueling was planned with a KC-135A of the 910th Air Refueling Squadron (radio call number Troubadour 14), piloted by Major Emil J. Chapla, from the SAC and Spanish Air Force base at Moron near Seville. This tanker, with 30,100 gallons of kerosene jet fuel aboard, was on temporary duty from its home at Bergstrom Air Force Base in Austin, Texas. Another B-52G (Tea 12) was being refueled by a KC-135A (Troubadour 12) in the same area at the same time.

The refueling over Palomares, in the province of Almeria, was expected to be a routine operation.[10] SAC bombers were refueled in the air at some point around the world every six minutes, day and night, by the fleet of about 700 KC-135 Stratotankers. Since 1959, more than 750,000 aerial refueling hookups had been carried out with only one known accident — a B-52 carrying nuclear bombs and a KC-135 had collided over Kentucky in October 1959. These nuclear bombs fortunately had been recovered intact. On this 17th day of January at 1022 Spanish time (0922Z — Zulu time),[11] however, a second and more serious refueling accident occurred.

The "History of Flight" section of the USAF Accident/Incident Report of the B-52 and KC-135 collision, which is the official USAF summary of the accident, follows:

> B-52G #58-256 (Tea 16), assigned to the 68th Bombardment Wing, Seymour Johnson AFB, North Carolina, and KC-135 #61-273 (Troubadour 14), assigned to the 97th Bombardment Wing, Blytheville AFB, Arkansas (on TDY — temporary duty — to the Spanish Tanker Task Force, Moron AB, Spain), collided and crashed at approximately 0920Z, 17 January 1966, while participating in air refueling operations in the Saddle Rock Air Refueling Area, Spain, 256° track.
>
> The mission was a scheduled indoctrination [training] flight (SAC OPORD 23-66, Chrome Dome Sorties 71 and 72), approximately 22 + 50 hours in duration for the B-52 and

Typical refueling of a B-52 Stratofortress from a KC-135 Stratotanker.

approximately 1 + 30 hours for the KC-135. Two air refuelings were scheduled, the first in the Golden Spur and the second in the Saddle Rock Area.

The crew of Tea 16 consisted of Capt. Charles J. Wendorf, [serial number] FR66865 (aircraft commander); 1st Lt. Richard J. Rooney, FV3131639 (copilot); Capt. Ivens Buchanan, FV3023677 (radar navigator); 1st Lt. Stephen S. Montanus, FV3139365 (navigator); 1st Lt. George J. Glesner, FV3122847 (substitute electronic warfare officer, as the regular EWO was on duty not involving flying [DNIF]); Tech. Sgt. Ronald P. Snyder, AF23914516 (gunner); and Maj. Larry G. Messinger, FV764067 (staff pilot).

The crew of Troubadour 14, TDY to the Spanish Tanker Task Force from the 340th Bombardment Wing, 910th Air Refueling Squadron, Bergstrom AFB, Texas, were Maj. Emil J. Chapla, FV803557 (aircraft commander); Capt. Paul R. Lane, FV306-4432 (copilot); Capt. Leo E. Simmons, FV3104001 (navigator); and Master Sgt. Lloyd G. Potolicchio, AF32960258 (boom operator).

A general Chrome Dome briefing was conducted at 1600Z, 24 December 1965, and pre-takeoff briefing at 2030Z, 16 January 1966, for the B-52 crew. The KC-135 crew received a general briefing at 0900Z, 15 January 1966, and pre-takeoff briefing at 0725Z, 17 January 1966. Tea 16 was scheduled to lead the two-ship formation the first half of the mission. Preflight of the B-52 was normal with the exception of number one UHF (ultra high frequency) radio malfunction and an oil-pressure-transmitter malfunction. As a result of the radio maintenance, Tea 16 took off eleven minutes late.

The mission progressed to the first air refueling with timing maintained within the prescribed block. Tea 16 reported that his autopilot would not maintain precise headings and exact altitude. The formation was on time at the Golden Spur ARCP [aerial refueling convergence point] at 0528Z. Tea 16 refueled using autopilot with Troubadour 13 and 11. End of air refueling track was approximately 0615Z. Briefed on-load was taken without an inadvertent disconnect. After completion of air refueling, Tea 16 changed from lead position to wing position.

The second air refueling was to be in the Saddle Rock Area with two KC-135 aircraft operating out of Moron AB, Spain. The other B-52 (Tea 12) was still in the lead position and accomplished the rendezvous. The weather in the refueling area was calm with no turbulence. Number two tanker, KC-135 #61-273, suggested that a higher formatting speed be used, and the tanker aircraft commander advised the B-52 Tea 16 that he would have limited breakaway capability due to a high gross weight. A rendezvous was accomplished and the initial approach to the tanker was normal to approximately one-half mile.

The B-52 apparently continued to close and a collision resulted. The B-52 pitched down and left, followed by a large explosion. The B-52 appeared to break up in the air following the explosion but the KC-135 continued ahead, shaking, for a very short distance. There was an explosion; then it pitched over into a descent and exploded again about 1600 feet above the ground and again on contacting the ground.

Both B-52 pilots ejected successfully. The B-52 radar navigator ejected and was burned as he encountered a fire ball immediately after ejection. Lieutenant Rooney, crew copilot, riding in the IN (instructor navigator) seat, bailed out through the radar navigator's hatch. The B-52 navigator ejected at a very low altitude just prior to the ground impact of the cockpit section. He was killed by impacting the ground approximately 25 yards away from the cockpit section. The B-52 radar navigator also failed to separate from the seat, but his chute deployed and he received a back injury from landing in his seat. The gunner and EWO did not eject and were fatally injured in the crash. All three pilots of the B-52 landed in the sea and were picked up by fishing boats. Both the radar navigator and the navigator landed on shore. Most of the wreckage of both aircraft is on land; however, two large pieces of B-52 wreckage were observed to fall into the sea. All crew members of the KC-135 received fatal injuries as the result of fire or ground impact.[12]

A 1975 report by the Defense Nuclear Agency provides a DoD summary of the collision:

On the morning of 17 January 1966, two Operation Chrome Dome B-52Gs, Tea 12 and Tea 16, rendezvoused with two KC-135As, Troubadour 12 and Troubadour 14, in the Saddle Rock refueling area at 31,000 feet. At approximately 0922Z the boom operator in Troubadour 12, while refueling Tea 12, reported to his pilot that he had observed fire balls and what appeared to be a center wing section in a flat spin. This report of disaster was the first of many dealing with the accident and its aftermath. Tea 16 and Troubadour 14 had collided while engaged in the final stages of hookup for refueling. Other aircraft, on other days, and at other places had collided in midair. Tea 16, however, was carrying four nuclear weapons. The events summarized in this report were the direct result of that aircraft accident involving nuclear weapons.

The crews of the other B-52 and KC-135 could not immediately determine the source of the falling debris. Troubadour 12 completed the refueling (10-12 minutes) of Tea 12 and then returned to the Palomares area to provide reconnaissance. Attempts to communicate with Troubadour 14 by radio were unsuccessful. Subsequently descending to 4,000 feet, Troubadour 12 sighted unidentifiable burning wreckage and, later, what appeared to be the tail section of a B-52. Other reports reached the Command Post at Moron AB from passing Spanish ships, a British ship, and a civil airliner. The Spanish Guardia Civil (Government Police) began reporting parachute sightings and the status of survivors. When these reports were radioed to Moron AB and passed to Torrejon, the full impact of the accident became apparent.

Eleven men were involved in the collision, four as crew members of the KC-135 and seven on the B-52. Of the four survivors, all from the B-52 crew, Captain Buchanan was the only one to come down on land. He was aided by Spanish residents and taken in the pickup truck of Senor Mañuel Gonzales Navarro to the Clinic Jacinto Gonzales in Vera, about seven kilometers distant. Captain Wendorf and Lieutenant Rooney were picked up by the fishing boat *Dorita,* Bartolome Roldan Martinez, master. Major Messinger was recovered by the fishing boat *Augustin y Rosa,* Alfonso Orts, master.

Both boats put into Aguilas, a nearby port, where the three survivors were taken to the local hospital and treated. Later that afternoon they were transferred to San Javier, a Spanish Air Force Base about 117 miles up the coast, and from that point were evacuated to Torrejon. Captain Buchanan, the most seriously injured of the four survivors, was treated at Vera and transferred by civil ambulance to San Javier and evacuated to Torrejon.

Seven of the men were killed as a result of the accident. Members of the Spanish Guardia Civil, under command of Capt. Isidoro Calin, took charge at the accident site. Remains were recovered and placed in caskets. (In the face of tragedy, people-to-people response lightens our load. On the evening of the accident the remains of the victims were brought to the Town Hall of Cuevas del Almanzora, northeast of Palomares. There, among burning candles, services were held by a Spanish priest. General Wilson received the remains and they were transported to San Javier and from there to Torrejon.) Seven bodies were identified by the afternoon of 18 January with the help of dental and other records. The remains were returned to the United States on 20 January.[13]

The doomed Tea 16 had a heading 256 degrees; the accident occurred about two miles inland over the coast of Palomares.

Major Messinger, the staff pilot, was flying the B-52 from the cockpit's left seat, and Captain Wendorf was in the right seat. A narrow corridor, with stairs, connected the cockpit with the aft double-level quarters for the rest of the crew. The electronic warfare operator, Lieutenant Glessner, and the gunner, Technical Sergeant Snyder, were at their upper-level work stations, the cockpit level. The navigator, Lieutenant Montanus, and the radar navigator, Captain Buchanan, were at their lower-level work stations. The copilot, Lieutenant Rooney, was sitting in the instructor navigator's seat, located in the lower level. The crew members, except for the pilots with their cockpit windows, did not have windows at their work stations.

Major Messinger, who had dropped bombs from B-17s over Europe in World War II and from B-29s over Korea, had on this fateful day throttled the B-52 back to 260 knots cruising speed at a 30,500-foot refueling altitude. The rate of closure of the B-52 and the KC-135 increased when the B-52 got within about 300 yards of the refueling tanker. There was then a call from the boom operator of the tanker: "You are going to have an over-run." Then Major Messinger put the nose of the aircraft in a slight descent. At this time, the nose of the B-52 was about even with the rear edge of the tanker's wings where they joined the fuselage.

Suddenly, a small explosion occurred, perhaps resulting from the tanker's fueling boom going through the B-52's wing, and Tea 16 pitched down. A bigger explosion and bright light followed, which blew off part of the front of the B-52.

Major Messinger ejected from the aircraft about this time. He grabbed the yellow ejection handles, located on each armrest, and the plane's hatch went off. Pulling up on the handles, Messinger shot out of the aircraft, then pulled the rip cord to open his parachute. Messinger was the first crew member to exit the plane. The offshore winds at the crash altitude were about 110 knots; these high winds drifted him out to sea. After descending into the water, Messinger untangled himself from his para-chute and got into the dinghy attached to his chute apparatus. He was picked up about eight miles offshore by the fishing boat *Augustin y Rosa.*

Captain Buchanan was the second crew member to eject after the colli-sion. His ejection seat worked fine exiting the plane, but unluckily he met a fireball head-on immediately after leaving the B-52. He then went into a flat spin and could not get out of it. Buchanan pulled out the rip cord of his parachute and wrapped it around his left hand to be sure the chute came out. But he could not separate from his ejection seat due to a mal-function, and the additional weight of the seat caused him to land on the shore at high speed. Buchanan's back was injured from the jolt of the impact, and he was unconscious for a few minutes. He was badly burned from the fireball and had a broken shoulder.

Captain Wendorf, age 29, had logged 2,500 flying hours, 2,100 in B-52s. He was the aircraft commander but was flying in the right seat as Messinger was acting as pilot at the time. With the initial pitch of the air-plane, Wendorf was thrown forward and hit his head on the control col-umn. He punched out of the damaged B-52 when it looked as if the ground was coming up fast. Immediately out of the airplane, he separated from the ejection seat and his parachute opened, but it was burned and tangled. He managed to untangle the shroud lines — the cords that suspended the harness from the canopy — so that the parachute inflated more fully just before water impact, but he still suffered a broken arm and was burned on the neck. Wendorf floated in the water for about 20 minutes before being picked up about two miles offshore by the fishing boat *Dorita.*

Lieutenant Rooney was sitting in the instructor navigator's seat and had no view of the collision. Per typical procedure, he had strapped on his parachute before the refueling (he had no ejection seat) and was wearing his helmet and mask, on normal oxygen. The first indication that anything was wrong was a sudden downward thrust of the plane. Something hit the aircraft or exploded just behind the electronic warfare officer's seat.

The decompression from Buchanan's ejection almost took Rooney's helmet off, disconnecting his mask. Thrown up on his feet at the first lurch of the B-52, he grabbed the stairway with one hand and the left-hand panel of the aircraft with the other. Then there was a muffled explosion, and an additional violent explosion threw him forward.

Rooney went past the hatch and slammed into the radar panel. The gravity force was strong, causing him to start crawling along the side of the panel, grasping instruments along the right side. Rooney finally reached the hatch and pulled himself halfway through. The wind blast was violent, and he was unable to move until the aircraft attitude changed very abruptly; he then rolled the rest of the way out of the plane. A tremendous explosion and a flash of light above him occurred as he fell. Something went whistling by in flames, probably an engine pod. Rooney was burned slightly by the trailing fire.

 He pulled his parachute's rip cord at about 14,000 feet, and his 24-foot-diameter canopy inflated as designed so that he hit the water at a low velocity. He went underwater a few feet and came right back up. After about 30 minutes, swimming to keep warm, he was picked up by the fishing boat *Dorita.*

The B-52 navigator, electronic warfare officer, and gunner tragically did not survive the accident. Lieutenant Montanus, the navigator, ejected and was found on the ground strapped in his heavy seat. Lieutenant Glessner and Sergeant Snyder probably could not eject from the B-52 due to the proximity of the boom penetration to their upper-crew stations and the resulting instantaneous explosion and fire.

As the official reports noted, none of the four men aboard the fueling tanker survived the accident. Flames rapidly raced from the burning and breaking-up B-52 up the boom to the KC-135 fuel tanks, torching off 30,000 gallons of jet fuel with a violent explosion.

Nuclear Community Alerted

As noted in the Defense Nuclear Agency 1975 report, the boom operator of the second KC-135A, Troubadour 12, while refueling the lead B-52G, Tea 12, had reported to his pilot that he had observed fireballs and a center wing section in a flat spin.[14] After refueling, Troubadour 12 descended to 4,000 feet over Palomares and reported burning wreckage and the B-52 tail section.

Major General Delmar E. Wilson, Commander of the 16th Air Force based in Torrejon, was immediately notified; he then passed the report to Major General Donald W. Eisenhart at SAC headquarters, Offutt Air Force Base, Omaha, Nebraska. Eisenhart in turn notified General John D. Ryan, SAC Commander. These messages set the Broken Arrow (the code term used in notifications of nuclear accidents) response system in motion.

At 0705 Washington time, an hour and a half after the accident, a messenger from the White House Situation Room brought a note into President Lyndon B. Johnson's bedroom, where he was having breakfast.[15] The President reached for the telephone and called Secretary of Defense Robert S. McNamara. "Is there any danger of an explosion?" he asked McNamara.

"We doubt it," was the answer.

"Do everything possible to find the nuclear weapons," the President replied.

Major General Stanley J. Donovan, Head of the Joint United States Military Advisory Group (JUSMAG) in Madrid and commander of all American forces in Spain as well as the senior U.S. representative to the Spanish military, called on General Augustin Munoz Grandes, Chief of the Spanish General Staff, and informed him of the accident. He also briefed the Spanish Air Minister, Lieutenant General José Maria LaCall E. Larriaga. The Torrejon Command Post notified U.S. Spanish Ambassador Angier Biddle Duke, who reported the accident to other Spanish authorities.

At 1125Z, only two hours after the collision,[16] the Joint Nuclear Accident Coordinating Center (JNACC) at Kirtland Air Force Base, New Mexico, received word of the situation. The JNACC was a joint Department of Defense and Atomic Energy Commission organization, charged with coordinating assistance for recovery from nuclear accidents. It had ready access to the technical capabilities of the atomic community centered in Albuquerque.

At 1136Z, General Wilson and three members of his staff departed Torrejon by T-39 command jet — a twin-engine North American Sabrejetliner — and surveyed the accident site from the air, landing at San Javier, the Spanish air force base about 117 miles up the coast from Palomares, at 1230Z.

At 1134Z, a C-97 departed Torrejon with 33 members of the Disaster Control Team — a unit already organized by 16th Air Force for disasters such as this — and three accident investigation personnel, and arrived at San Javier at 1240Z.

At 1221Z, a Disaster Control Team under Major General A. J. Beck, Deputy Chief of Staff, Material, SAC, left Omaha and arrived at San Javier at 0114Z, 18 January, and at the accident scene at 0630Z.

The Air Force Nuclear Safety Directorate at Kirtland AFB advised the JNACC that a team of four of their staff (headed by Colonel William E. Gernert) had air transport to Spain and offered space to other response personnel. Representatives of the JNACC, the Atomic Energy Commission (D. J. Hart), the Los Alamos Scientific Laboratory (W. H. Chambers and D. F. Evans), and Sandia Corporation (S. V. Asselin) were alerted; they departed Albuquerque on the aircraft at 1800Z. By the evening of 17 January, 49 United States personnel had arrived at Palomares to assess the sobering task that lay before them.

The Press

The first and all subsequent news releases of the accident required considerable coordination between the Department of Defense, the State Department, and the Spanish government.[17] At 0945Z (23 minutes after the accident), the 16th Air Force Director of Information, Lieutenant Colonel Barnett Young, was informed of the collision, and within five minutes the news had been relayed to his SAC counterpart in the United States.

Before the JUSMAG and the U.S. Information Service (USIS) could be notified, the Associated Press (AP) correspondent from Madrid called. He had already received information on the crash from a correspondent in Vera and wanted more details. By 1130Z, seven more queries had been received: from United Press International (UPI), Westinghouse Broadcasting Corporation, Europa Press, Reuters, American Broadcasting Company (ABC), *Stars and Stripes,* and the public relations office of European Command U.S. (EUCOM), Camp de Loges, France. But very little information was available at Torrejon.

General Ryan at SAC headquarters gave permission for Torrejon to release the information on the home bases of the aircraft and that the crews were flying a refueling mission on a routine training flight. The names of the known survivors were released as they became available; however, in conformance with policy, the names of the casualties could not be given until the next of kin had been notified.

But the news agencies did not wait for official releases, and the first dispatch on the teletype receiver at Torrejon was from UPI at the Hague at 1130Z; the Dutch vessel *Willem Koerts* had radioed that two jet fighters collided in the Cartegena area (between Vera and San Javier) with one ditching in the Mediterranean and the other continuing its flight.

The AP released five news dispatches from 1230Z to 1805Z with considerable details: four parachutes were seen descending, the survivor (Buchanan) had been interviewed, and the Spanish police had recovered four charred bodies. None of the dispatches indicated whether the B-52 carried nuclear arms. The AP's 1805Z release listed the names of the four known survivors; these names had been given to both the AP and UPI by the 16th Air Force.

Because Buchanan had been interviewed by UPI, Strategic Air Command stated that valid questions about Buchanan could be answered to avoid embarrassment to the United States and the government of Spain. But that evening, SAC ruled that no press interviews would be permitted at Torrejon even though reporters were aware that three of the four crew members had been returned to the Torrejon hospital.

Meanwhile, SAC was busy preparing a release. The draft was read over the telephone to the 16th Air Force at 1530Z. However, it could not be made public until it was cleared with USIS, JUSMAG, the U.S. Embassy, and the Spanish government. At 2030Z, 11 hours after the accident, this first joint Department of Defense and State Department statement was released from Spain to the AP and UPI:

> A B-52 bomber from the 68th Bomb Wing at Seymour Johnson AFB, North Carolina, and a KC-135 Tanker from the 910th Aerial Refueling Squadron at Bergstron AFB, Texas, crashed

today southwest of Cartegena, Spain, during scheduled air operations. There are reports of some survivors from the crews of the aircraft. An AF Accident Investigation Team has been dispatched to the scene. Additional details will be available as the investigation progresses.[18]

Chapter 2

Three Bombs Found

$\mathcal{T}$he mid-air collision and the resulting bomb search would drastically change the lifestyles of the inhabitants of Palomares.

W. R. Barton

Fishing boats moored at Garrucha, the first port southeast of Palomares.

THE FIRST AMERICANS arrived in Palomares, ready to determine the seriousness of the situation involving the nuclear weapons. Their priority concerned people: the crew members of the aircraft and the residents of the village.[19] After General Wilson had seen to the condition of the surviving airmen in Aguilas and the remains of the deceased in Cuevas, he was assured by local authorities at Palomares that no injuries had been sustained by the populace.

The mid-air collision and the resulting bomb search would drastically change the lifestyles of the inhabitants of Palomares. This remote, sleepy village, population about 2,000, is on the southeast coast of Spain in the province of Almeria.[20] A few miles southeast of Palomares is the fishing village of Garrucha and the Moorish village of Mojacar. A few miles northeast is the tiny fishing village of Villaricos (250 residents), and about 20 miles up the coast northeast is the major fishing city of Aguilas (population 15,000). A rutted, twisting dirt road, four and a half miles long heading northwest, connected Palomares to the outside world, to the ancient Roman city of Vera (population 6,000).

The land in Palomares had been mined for centuries for silver, copper, lead, and other minerals. Smelters in the hills were connected by elevated flues that brought sea breezes to the smelters. The mines gave out early in this century, and the mining legacy left the Palomares area with open shafts, fields of slag, and crumbling flues, pillars, and roofless walls. The presence of these diggings was to play a part in the search for the missing bomb.

Small adobe houses, clustered in groups of three or so in the village, had open-air extended roofs where the cows, horses, or chickens could seek shelter from the hot sun. Palomares is sufficiently arid that its only industry, agriculture, depends on deep-well irrigation. Relying on this irrigation, the village had been able to enjoy a little prosperity.

Electricity, provided by a local generator, came to Palomares in 1958, and with it, radios and a few television sets. These modern media, which were to carry the Palomares story to the world, involved the people of that *barriada* (hamlet) in the diplomatic and propaganda maneuverings of the nuclear powers.

The people of Palomares were farmers and farm laborers, but the waters off the Palomares coast were the harvest grounds of many fishermen from nearby ports and villages. These people, after playing the major role in the rescue of the surviving airmen, were to be excluded from parts of their

Typical transportation in Palomares.

Village children.

The impact area of the #1 bomb at Palomares, 1966.   *Bob Reed*

fishing grounds by the extensive underwater salvage operation that was to follow.

One can only imagine the response of individuals on the ground to the collision of the B-52 and KC-135 30,000 feet above them. The refueling operations were not new to the residents of Palomares; many "hookups" had been witnessed on other occasions. The 17th of January, however, was different. Some saw the collision; others looked up only when they heard the explosion. What they all saw was the burning aircraft wreckage falling about their village and farm plots. The B-52 had broken apart at high altitude, but the KC-135 had remained fairly intact as it plummeted to earth; it apparently exploded just before ground contact (about 1,600 feet) and again on contact. Engines, wing sections, gear, and other smaller pieces fell about the countryside, in backyards and open fields. The debris pattern on land was spread over several square miles. The B-52 tail section landed in the bed of the dry Almanzora River, about one mile from the village.

Father Serraro, a circuit priest from Cuevas del Almanzora who tended to Palomares parishioners, suggested that "the hand of God" had protected the village. Aside from being frightened, no person or animal was injured, nor was any structure damaged, other than for broken windows and the like.

A Successful Search

Though the remaining daylight time was limited when General Wilson and the Disaster Control Team arrived at the scene on the 17th, they immediately recognized that this would be a major recovery operation. The task of cleaning up the debris would clearly require several weeks. That evening was spent in planning the work for the next day, which set a pattern that was followed for what was to be the next 80 days.

Some members of the response force — wearing, of course, masks and protective clothing — had performed initial radiation surveys, predominantly around the areas of major wreckage. These surveys indicated that, thankfully, there had been no nuclear explosion. But somewhere, in the gathering darkness, four nuclear weapons had to be located. There were many stories told by the local Spaniards who had seen parachutes with projectiles attached, but few of the Americans could understand the language.

Just before dark, Sergeant Raymond Howe, who had been conducting radiation monitoring of some of the wreckage, learned of a possible spotting of a weapon from a member of the Guardia Civil (the Spanish government police). That report led the Disaster Control Team to its first find, about 900 feet from the beach and a little over a mile southeast of the village.

The weapon had been only slightly damaged on impact. It apparently had fallen against a soft, high bank and rolled to the bank's base. Radiation checks were negative. The team decided to leave render-safe procedures — employed to ensure that a weapon's firing system is disarmed — until morning, as it was by then too dark to accomplish the task.

Air Force guards were posted at this weapon, referred to as #1. (The weapons were given numbers in the order in which they were found.) Team spirit rose at the relative ease of the #1 find and at its good condition. But darkness and the rugged terrain in another search area a mile west of the village made it necessary to postpone the search for the other three bombs until morning.

General Wilson decided to bring personnel in — American and Spanish, but mostly from the 16th Air Force — from the two Spanish bases at Moron and Torrejon. Movement started at 0100Z on 18 January from Moron, followed by a second convoy at 0310Z; the first of the two convoys started from Torrejon at 0137Z and the second at 0202Z. A total of 126 United States personnel were transported to Palomares, a 12- to

14-hour drive, in six buses. Accompanying the convoy were an ambulance, a van, and a truck carrying bedding, food, water, and radios.

At first light on the 18th, Wilson's Disaster Control Team gathered at the B-52 tail section in the dry bed of the Almanzora River, which was to be used as a command post. All available personnel were pressed into the search effort. Hopes were high that the remaining weapons would be found as quickly as the first one had been.

The searchers were not disappointed; by 0930 hours (times are local unless indicated otherwise), the second weapon was located. Unlike #1, however, #2 had been substantially damaged upon impact. Part of the weapon's high explosive had detonated, but, as designed, no nuclear detonation had taken place. Portions of the weapon were in a crater about 20 feet in diameter and six feet in depth. Other parts of the weapon assembly were found as far away as 100 yards.

Weapon render-safe procedures were not required. The primary concern with #2 was the plutonium contamination that had been released by the high-explosive detonation. Radiation detection equipment indicated the presence of significant alpha contamination — nuclear radiation — in the area.

The search continued. At approximately 1030 hours, one hour after #2 had been located, #3 was discovered within the limits of the village of Palomares. Its high explosive had also detonated, but again there had been no nuclear detonation. Parts of the weapon were strewn to distances of 500 yards. Plutonium contamination was also present at the site.

The 2,250-pound B28 bombs (145 inches long and 22 inches in diameter) that had fallen from the crippled B-52 were each equipped with a complicated four-parachute system, designed by the Parachute Branch, Wright-Patterson Air Force Base, Dayton, Ohio, and Sandia Corporation. The parachute pack on each was 48 inches long and weighed 275 pounds, and the chutes had canopy diameters of 30 inches, 4 feet, 16 feet, and 64 feet.

Used properly, the 4-foot-diameter guide surface parachute was deployed for the retarded fusing option. It then deployed the 16-foot-diameter ribbon parachute that decelerated the bomb for two seconds. The 16-foot parachute was then cut loose from the bomb and pulled the 64-foot parachute pack out of the bomb, which inflated and decelerated the bomb to a velocity of about 28 feet per second at impact. This high parachute drag increased the time of flight of the bomb, which allowed time for the

Release of a B28 bomb with 64-foot-diameter parachute at Sandia's Tonopah Test Range, Nevada.

delivery aircraft to escape the effects of the nuclear explosion. And because the bomb was unstable with its small fins, a 30-inch-diameter guide surface parachute was used to stabilize it for the high-altitude (free-fall) delivery option. (The Sandia design of high-performance parachutes for laydown nuclear bombs is discussed in a book that I coauthored for NATO, *Design and Testing of High Performance Parachutes*.)[21]

But because the B28s were torn from the B-52's bomb rack in a random fashion at aircraft breakup, any of the parachutes could have been deployed. The 16-foot parachute opened on the #1 bomb, which hit the ground at about 135 feet per second with minimal damage to the bomb.

The #2 bomb tumbled free-fall (no parachute was deployed), impacting the ground at about 390 feet per second; it was found with part of the bomb rack still attached. This high-impact velocity caused the high explosive (HE) to detonate, which scattered plutonium dust over many acres. Case fragments and about ten pounds of HE were found within 300 feet of its crater.

The 16-foot parachute deployed, but was damaged, on the #3 bomb. The bomb impacted the ground at about 194 feet per second. This high-impact velocity also caused an HE explosion that scattered plutonium dust over many acres, along with approximately 80 pounds of HE and plastics within 100 feet of its crater. Weapon parts were strewn up to 400 yards.

One may wonder why nuclear detonation did not occur, since the bombs hit the ground with such high impact. An explanation of the design of these particular bombs is thus in order. The plutonium in the primary — the fission trigger, or first stage, of a multistage thermonuclear weapon — is surrounded by many high-explosive lenses. These lenses are symmetrical segments (numbering, say, 40) of a thin spherical shell of HE — each segment of equal area with a detonator centered on the outer surface — which surrounds the uranium or plutonium nuclear material. When these HE lenses are detonated *simultaneously,* they implode the primary, which causes fusion of the weapon's secondary — a thermonuclear explosion. The high-impact velocity of the #2 and #3 bombs dropped over Palomares caused the lenses to explode, but *non-simultaneously,* which resulted in the low-order HE explosion. These nuclear bombs were designed to be one-point safe — that is, if the HE was initiated at a single point (at one lens), the design of the nuclear system ensured that the nuclear yield

The remains of the #2 B28 bomb after the impact detonation of its high explosive. The 16-foot ribbon parachute is attached to the 64-foot parachute pack, partially in bomb.

equivalent (the equivalent damage from a high explosive) was less than four pounds of TNT, with a probability of such an explosion not to exceed one in a million.

Surveying the Sites

The radiation surveys at Palomares were conducted by measuring radiation counts per minute (CPM) emitted by plutonium on the PAC-1S, the only alpha radiation detector available to measure plutonium contamination, which unfortunately suffered from an unusually high failure rate.[22] When the Palomares accident occurred, General Wilson stated that the U.S. Air Force was unprepared to provide adequate detection and monitoring for personnel when an aircraft accident happened involving plutonium weapons in a remote area of a foreign country. Yet the safety of the troops and the Spanish villagers from radiation exposure, and the plutonium cleanup, was dependent on the proper use of this only-available detector.

Randall Maydew holding the 16-foot ribbon parachute of the recovered #1 B28 bomb, in the National Atomic Museum, Albuquerque, New Mexico.

Walter J. Dickenman, Sandia National Laboratories

Historically, portable alpha radiation detectors have not been reliable for open terrain surveys. The problems with this instrumentation are inherent in the design and the characteristics of alpha particle radiation. The plutonium alpha particle has a very short range of travel in air (three to

The remains of the #3 B28 bomb after the impact detonation of its high explosive. From left to right, the 16-foot, 64-foot, and 30-inch-diameter parachutes can be seen.

The tail of the downed B-52 in the dry bed of the Almanzora River. Note the Air Force trucks and the village of Palomares in the background.

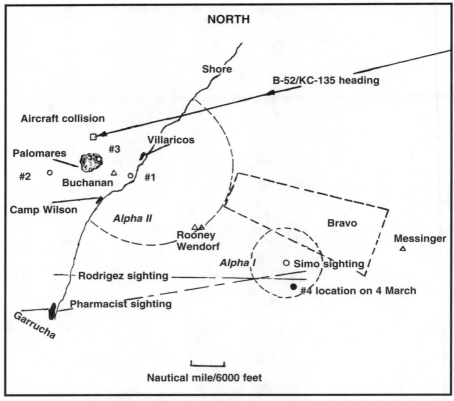

NORTH

Shore

B-52/KC-135 heading

Aircraft collision

Palomares   □◄   Villaricos
        #3

#2   ○   ○   #1
        Buchanan   △

Camp Wilson

        Alpha II   Bravo

                    △△
                    Rooney   Messinger
                    Wendorf   △

                    Alpha I   ○ Simo sighting

Rodrigez sighting ─────────────────

                                    ● #4 location on 4 March
Pharmacist sighting

Garrucha

        ┗━━━━━┛
        Nautical mile/6000 feet

Sketch of the accident scene and bomb recovery areas.

four cm) and cannot penetrate a blade of grass or a thin film of ground
moisture. Thus, the alpha detector must be positioned extremely close to
the surface to accurately detect alpha particle radiation — so close that
even in the hands of experienced personnel there is the danger that surface
irregularities (grass, rocks, etc.) will penetrate the extremely thin window
of the detector's wand and result in an erroneous reading.

By the evening of the day of the accident, 17 January, a small monitoring team equipped with PAC-1S detectors was at Palomares. Site locations
were numbered for identification purposes: Sites 1, 2, and 3 were the locations of the bomb impacts; Site 5 was the village of Palomares, between
and connecting Sites 2 and 3; and Site 6 was east of the riverbed near the
B-52 tail section impact site, a continuation of Site 3. For some unknown

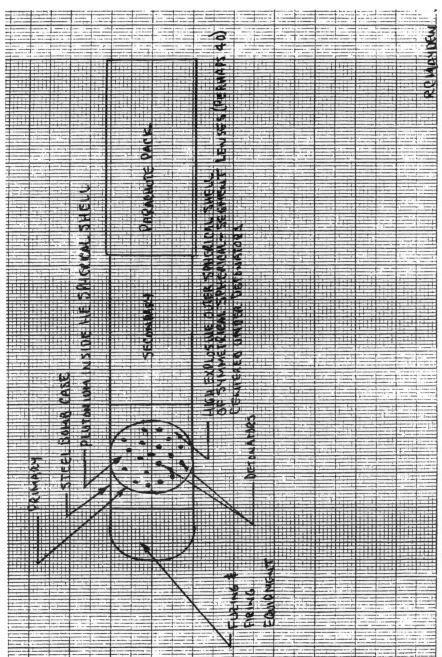

Schematic of a B28 bomb, illustrating high-explosive lenses.

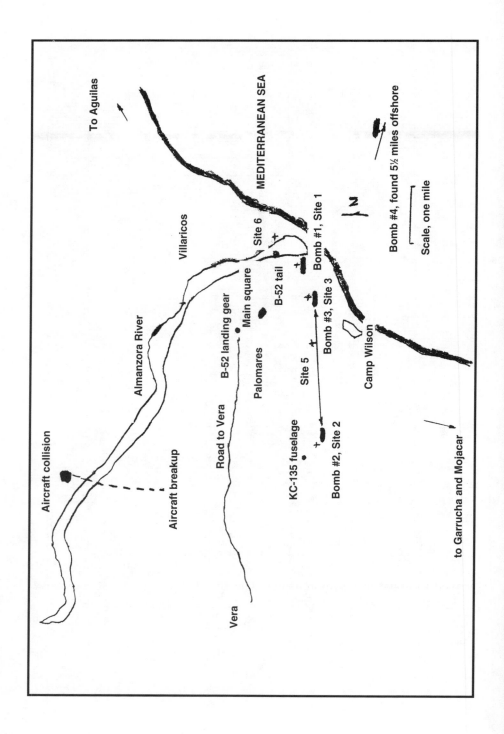

Colonel William E. Gernert, Air Force Nuclear Safety Directorate, and Doug Evans, Los Alamos, using the PAC-1S detector.

reason, there was no Site 4. The PAC-1S detectors found no contamination at Site 1, where Bomb #1 had been found and surveyed.

On 18 January, when Bombs #2 and #3 were located, the monitoring team, operating primarily in support of the 16th's Explosive Ordnance Disposal (EOD) personnel, found that alpha contamination was generally present in the area. At Site 2, the tail section of the weapon had been displaced some 250 feet by the detonation, and readings on this weapon section "pegged" the PAC-1S at 2,000,000 CPM.

On Wednesday, the 19th, the first attempt was made to define the contaminated areas, and the remainder of the Torrejon Hazard Survey Force arrived to assist in the monitoring. The first job was to assist Explosive Ordnance Disposal personnel in their task by providing local monitoring around the immediate crater areas. Radial line plots of the area were started at the same time. However, because of a shortage of personnel and PAC-1S detectors, all monitoring activity at Site 2 was stopped on 20 January. And because Site 3 was located at the edge of the village of Palomares, the potential political implications of this contamination were considered. The team was concerned about the villagers and their morale, and thus the monitoring was stopped for a while at this site as well. Four to five days of detailed monitoring had showed that the contamination extended into the valley below the crater created by the #3 bomb to a distance of about 4,500 feet; it included farms and cropland.

The Press

The Associated Press had asked about nuclear weapons on 17 January, but information concerning weapons was not available to them. Indeed, U.S. policy specified that nuclear weapon information could not be released. But by the afternoon of the 19th, radiation hazards and lost bombs were the subject of the day, and it was no longer possible to adhere to the policy of not discussing nuclear weapons. The Reuters's representative in Madrid called concerning a rumored "450 airmen with Geiger counters looking for nuclear material." ABC reported, also from Madrid, that "several hundred United States airmen combed the Spanish countryside today looking for — to quote — 'the nuclear weapon or weapons that were aboard the crashed B-52.'"

At 2105Z, SAC advised the 16th Air Force that two United Press International dispatches, both datelined 20 January, had been received. The lead paragraph of the first read:

> Residents of this tiny village (Palomares) waited nervously while the US Air Force searched for an atomic bomb carried by a nuclear bomber which crashed after colliding in the air with a KC-135 jet tanker.[23]

The story included the "no comment" statement of personnel at the site and at Torrejon and also mentioned that hundreds of airmen were hunting for a nuclear device. The reporter went on to say that the immediate crash site had been evacuated but the general area was not, and that about 50 Guardia Civil were preventing civilian entrance to the crash zone while the Americans hunted for some object.

The second article, written in a more personal style, started:

> Searching for a missing atom bomb is not exactly my idea of the best way to spend a holiday on the sunny coast of southern Spain.

The reporter explained his sources of information:

> I saw American airmen, some of them carrying Geiger coun-
> ters and many of them wearing radiation detection badges,
> scouring the area in the search for the missing bomb.
>
> I was stopped by a guard in the area. He asked me if I could
> speak Spanish and I said yes. Then he asked if I could go with
> him to a nearby bean field where a Spanish farmer was cutting
> his crop.
>
> The guard explained the Guardia Civil had been instructed to
> clear the area of all people because it was contaminated.
>
> After further questioning, the guard said one nuclear device
> was missing from the crashed B-52. . . .
>
> The guard said that two bombs were found during this first
> day's search in the arid, sparsely-vegetated hills and the last
> bomb was found on the beach.[24]

With UPI's extensive coverage throughout the world, the implications of these releases could not be ignored.

At 1230Z, 20 January, the second official USAF/SAC release was received at Madrid and distributed:

> The Strategic Air Command bomber which was engaged in
> a refueling operation off the coast of Spain, and suffered an
> accident with a KC-135 tanker, was carrying unarmed nuclear
> armament. Radiological surveys have established that there
> is no danger to public health or safety as a result of this acci-
> dent.[25]

The Spanish Air Ministry also issued a press release on 20 January:

> With reference to the air accident that occurred off the Span-
> ish coast in the province of Almeria, it has been determined that
> it was a collision between a tanker aircraft and a long-range
> American jet plane while a refueling operation was underway.
>
> The authorities and civilian personnel of that area went to
> help the crews and they managed to save four fliers and they
> helped put out the fires of what remained of the aircraft that col-

lided and which had fallen in the neighborhood of the villages of Vera and Palomares.

The last area, five kilometers in diameter, over which the debris was scattered and the recovery of elements of a secret military nature have made necessary the search and safety measures taken by this ministry in order to obtain full information and analyze the conclusions of flight safety procedures.

The Air Ministry appreciates the cooperation given by the local authorities and civilian personnel and their spontaneous and courageous help which made possible the assistance given and the work that is underway to complete the investigation with added safety.[26]

Chapter 3

Camp Wilson and the Intensified Search

ogistics for Operation Recovery was a major problem. The accident site had none of the essentials for support . . .

Ground searchers combing the fields of Palomares for the missing #4 bomb.

*W*ITH TENTS AND related equipment requisitioned from Gray Eagle stocks at Wheelus Air Base, Tripoli (Gray Eagle is the concept of prepositioning forward operating base assets in support of tactical air deployments), a temporary camp — a tent city called Camp Wilson — was established at the dry riverbed site by Wednesday, 19 January. Many activities were underway simultaneously at the camp, but the three top priorities were the search for the #4 bomb, decontamination, and the completion of the accident investigation. Each of these activities was supported by a fourth, the cleanup of aircraft and weapon debris.

By Friday the 21st, earth-moving equipment had leveled a more suitable area for the camp on higher, firmer ground three and a half miles east of Garrucha. This site lessened the dust problem and eliminated the potential of flash flooding in the dry arroyo of the original location. The 75-tent camp, with its helicopter landing area and motor pool, served until 3 April as a "forward base" for the specialized task of cleaning up the Spanish countryside.

The original Disaster Control Team from Torrejon had consisted of 33 members plus three accident investigation personnel. The number of on-site staff grew rapidly, reaching a peak of 681 by 31 January. Two-thirds of these were involved in either searching for the missing weapon or in cleaning up the debris, while the remaining were air police and communications, medical, claims, and other support personnel. Of these, 598 were U.S. Air Force, 64 U.S. Army, and 19 U.S. Navy personnel.

Except for some of the officers who were quartered in two hotels close to the accident scene, all personnel were housed in the tent city. Other staff at the camp site, although not housed there, were the approximately 126 Guardia Civil and the 39 Spanish personnel. They worked along with the Americans in the cleanup of the aircraft debris and in the camp kitchen.

Daytime temperatures reached as high as 80° to 90° F, but wind conditions and sea dampness, along with 40° to 45° night temperatures, made tent heaters necessary to avoid respiratory infections. Accordingly, kerosene heaters were in use by 3 February.

After the Gray Eagle equipment became available, hot meals were served. Daily courier flights from Torrejon to San Javier, with transfer to helicopters for air service into Palomares, permitted milk and fresh bread to be flown in along with the necessary rations. Some Guardia Civil and Spanish laborers, who worked with the Americans at the site, were also furnished meals.

The outdoor mess hall at Camp Wilson.

General Wilson's command tent.

But while Gray Eagle supplies provided immediate basic camp necessities and eased considerably the Operation Recovery effort — the informal name of the mission — normal Gray Eagle packaging for deployment did not allow easy access to specific items. For instance, when the operation required machetes, 60 cases might have to be opened to satisfy the requirement, as personnel didn't know which cases the machetes were in or how many were in each. In all, 306,853 pounds of Gray Eagle equipment were provided to Camp Wilson.

Logistics for Operation Recovery was a major problem. The accident site had none of the essentials for support, and Camp Wilson had no airstrip. Most of the materials were flown into San Javier and then trucked to the site, much over a very poor road network. During one period, 148 vehicles were involved in the mission, 21 by the unit at San Javier and 127 at Camp Wilson: supply and personnel vehicles, tank trucks and pumpers, road grading equipment, limb shredders, wreckers, forklifts, and tractors. These were augmented by commercial truck and rail as required.

Vehicle assets of the 16th Air Force were exhausted by the effort, and

Bill Barton of Sandia Corporation and Captain Isidora Calin of the Spanish Guardia Civil.
W. R. Barton

Bill Barton of Sandia getting a haircut at Camp Wilson.

requests went to other commands for support. A long-lived major quandary was equipment maintenance. The problem was aggravated by parts supply problems and the fact that vehicles in poor condition had been supplied by agencies involved. At one point in the operation, the 16th Air Force sent a "temporary duty" team to the United States to expedite the flow of supply parts.

The 16th Air Force requested and received aircraft assistance from several sources. The Army provided UH-1 helicopters (16th Air Force provided JP-4 fuel) to conduct search operations. Airlift consisted of tankers from Torrejon and Moron, theater aircraft, and unrestricted use of eight

Military Airlift Command (MAC) — the C-124 Globemaster and the C-130 Hercules — until they were released on 7 March by the 16th Air Force. In addition, MAC used three civilian Boeing 707s to deliver Operation Recovery equipment on four occasions. Tragically, one aircraft accident occurred during the recovery operation: a MAC C-124 crashed at Granada, Spain, on 12 February. The entire aircrew was killed and the logistic supplies, two buses, and lights for Camp Wilson were lost.

Communications, like logistics, was a "build it up" process. Although the Compania Telefonica National de España pointed with pride that "at a minimum, every village in Spain had at least one telephone," there was none at Palomares. The nearest phone was located at Vera, about ten miles distant; it took General Wilson 40 minutes to travel from Palomares to Vera and an hour's wait for a circuit. Priority was thus given to establish a Single Side Band (SSB) radio/telephone capability. These SSB units had been brought by the team arriving at Palomares on the evening of the accident. By 1859Z that night, communications were established with Torrejon, but secure communications were not available at that time, and Air Rescue cover aircraft had provided early relay communications service to San Javier.

The Spanish government, recognizing that San Javier would be heavily used for the operation, offered its air defense microwave system with a terminal at that base. A telephone connection to this system was established at San Javier on 18 January.

The next increment of communications capability came on-line at Camp Wilson on 22 January, providing a secure teletype service to Torrejon. This service was provided by United States personnel and mobile equipment of the Second Mobile Communications Group of Toul Rosieres Air Base, France. The circuit was relayed through Croughton, England. Several attempts were made by a second unit from the French base to establish direct communications from Palomares to Torrejon, but the quality of the service did not equal that of the Croughton link, and attempts were abandoned on 3 February.

General Wilson requested that at least two methods of communication be available in case one system failed. Even though the Spanish telephone/microwave system could provide service from Vera to Torrejon, a necessary but missing link was wire service from Palomares to Vera. At 1230Z, 22 January, a request for a land line to fill the gap and for an in-camp telephone system was initiated with U.S. Army support units in

Europe. By 2200Z, on 23 January, the Palomares-Vera line had been laid, and by the next morning the in-camp net had been installed.

Another communications service utilized was portable citizens band radios. The search operations covered considerable territory, and portable radios were used by the several teams that were spread over the area. For this purpose, as well as for all radio operations in the region, coordination was required with the Spanish government for allocation of frequencies. Authorization was received in all cases on a priority basis.

The Systems Analysis Team and Task Force 65

In order to bring as much expertise to the mission as possible, General Wilson requested that an analysis group be formed and furnished with all the data available at the site. Thus, the Systems Analysis Team (SAT) was born.

After Jack Howard's initial 22 January telephone call to Alan Pope at Sandia, the aerodynamics group in Albuquerque, of which I was a part, immediately started making computer trajectory calculations to predict the location of the #4 bomb.[27]

Our role, because we had helped design the complicated parachute system, was to estimate where the bomb had hit the earth, on land or sea. Everything about the mid-air collision had to be reconstructed — from B-52 altitude and true course to airspeed plus winds — in order to calculate trajectories for all four bombs.

There were many variables in the equations. For example, according to the KC-135 Stratotanker navigator, the estimated wind at the refueling altitude was about 110 knots blowing out to sea. Trajectory calculations indicated that if the 64-foot parachute was immediately deployed after the crash, the 110-knot wind would carry the missing bomb several miles seaward.

Sandia aerodynamicists and mathematicians Sam McAlees, Jr., Floyd Forsythe, William Pepper, and I formed the first study group to make calculations of the bomb trajectories. Some of the calculations required five to six hours of IBM 7090 and Control Data 3600 computer time for just one bomb trajectory. This work was coordinated with the Directorate of Nuclear Safety at Kirtland Air Force Base, which was receiving messages and data from General Wilson's staff at Palomares.

The initial studies were completed the weekend of 22-23 January so that on Monday, Sam McAlees could brief Jack Howard and military offi-

cials at the Pentagon on the results of the preliminary trajectory calculations. These calculations served as the basis for the initial planning of the
impending Navy sea search. Additional ballistic studies, based on new
information, were started that day by Bill Barton and Ira Holt, and Lou
Feltz plotted the results of the calculations on charts.

The estimated impact areas for the missing bomb were forwarded to
General Wilson's staff on the Palomares beach by secret telegraph.
Because of special paperwork required at both ends and misunderstand-
ings regarding terminology, aerodynamics, and the like, these secret communications to and from Camp Wilson were slow and cumbersome.

After contacting Alan Pope at Sandia, Jack Howard next requested
search and recovery help from the Navy through Dr. Robert W. Morris,
Assistant Secretary of the Navy for Research and Development. In
response, on Sunday, 23 January, Admiral David L. McDonald, Chief of
Naval Operations (CNO), established AIRCRAFT SALVOPS MED (Aircraft Salvage Operations Mediterranean) and directed mobilization of
Navy resources to assist in the search and recovery of the lost nuclear
weapon. Because the Navy was responsible for the disposal of explosive
ordnance discovered within the ocean, the task of locating the missing
weapon was given a high priority.

The Chief of Naval Operations's order resulted in two primary actions,
one on-site and the other within the naval establishment in Washington.
First, Task Force 65 (TF-65) was organized from the assets of the Sixth
Fleet. Rear Admiral William S. Guest, USN, Deputy Commander, Naval
Strike and Support Forces, Southern Europe, was selected as the Task
Force Commander (CTF); he arrived at Camp Wilson on 24 January from
his station in Naples.

After a briefing in General Wilson's tent, Admiral Guest went up for an
aerial survey of the area and then boarded a rubber boat with several Navy
divers for the trip to the minesweeper USS *Skill*, his first flagship. A few
hours later, the USS *MacDonough*, a guided missiles frigate, arrived; the
Admiral transferred to the frigate, and Task Force 65 was formally consti-
tuted. The Task Force continued to grow in ships, men, and sophisticated
equipment.

At the same time, a Technical Advisory Group (TAG) was formed
under the chairmanship of Rear Admiral Leroy V. Swanson, USN, Assistant Chief of Naval Operations (Fleet Operations)/Director Fleet Operations Division. The TAG consisted of representatives of those elements

within or close to the naval establishment who were most knowledgeable in the field of deep submergence capabilities and environmental problems; the members were Rear Admiral O. D. Waters, Oceanographer of the Navy; Captain E. J. Snyder, Jr., Special Assistant to the Assistant Secretary of the Navy (R & D); Captain W. F. Searle, Jr., Supervisor of Salvage, U.S. Navy; Dr. John P. Craven, Chief Scientist, Deep Submergence Systems Project; and Rear Admiral (Ret.) E. C. Stephan, Submergence Systems Review Group. They met formally for the first time on 24 January in Washington, D.C.

The mission of Task Force 65 and the Technical Advisory Group, as directed by the Chief of Naval Operations, was to support and "conduct coordinated surface and subsurface operations in the vicinity of Palomares, Spain, in order to detect, identify, and recover material associated with the aircraft collision."[28] This task was to keep both groups working at maximum effort for the next 75 days — until the lost weapon was found, placed in its shipping container, and returned to the United States.

The military establishment was prepared for such emergencies or accidents with contingency directives to be instituted through the chain of command. But before the accident at Palomares, no weapon had been lost at sea in what could be termed foreign territorial waters. Consequently, the normal chain of command was modified to include representatives of Secretary of the Navy Paul H. Nitze and Secretary of State Dean Rusk.

Once the available information regarding the Palomares accident had been passed to Task Force 65 by the 16th Air Force, the at-sea operations proceeded with little dependence upon the land operation. From the outset, naval participation was geared to the assumption that the fourth nuclear weapon was in fact lost at sea, so that the same eventual conclusion by the Air Force had little direct effect on the tempo of operations of the sea searchers.

The development of Task Force 65 was slow and at best piecemeal. Very early in the effort, minimum requirements for the Task Force were estimated, and ships at least partially equipped for the specialized operations were assigned; however, not every ship was able to sail to the scene right away. As the sea search effort continued with forces immediately available from Sixth Fleet, the Technical Advisory Group laid the highest priority upon procuring the military and civilian expertise in the field of deep-sea recovery as well as much of the equipment and instrumentation suggested by these experts. As personnel arrived by sea and air, initially from the complements of the ships on station off Palomares, Admiral Guest began to fill the slots of his final staff organization.

Admiral McDonald had directed that full and precise documentation of AIRCRAFT SALVOPS MED would be required should the search be unsuccessful. These records would provide proof of the effort expended and justification for terminating the search short of success. In addition, this documentation would be useful for the development of procedures, vehicles, and equipment to handle future emergencies.

To accomplish this task, a tactical analysis group, composed of four naval officers and three civilian analysts, was ordered to report to Admiral Guest by the middle of February. It should be noted that all four of the naval officers were qualified submariners, an appropriate selection because Admiral Guest was an aviator and not experienced in matters pertaining to the search for and recovery of objects on the ocean's floor. With the addition of these seven personnel, Admiral Guest at last had an adequate functional staff. The director of the group was assigned as TF-65 Operations Officer on the staff, thus providing the submarine experience previously missing from the Task Force organization.

Although not formally depicted on the organization charts, official liaison was established with a small Spanish naval detachment in Aguilas. It was this group that ordered the available vessels in the area to proceed and assist immediately after the accident. They were charged with supporting Task Force 65 in maintaining the integrity of the search area and search operations. On one occasion, when a French salvage ship showed up in the middle of the Task Force, the Spanish authorities were asked to use their influence to remove the unwanted guest from the area of operations. The French ship complied. The Spanish naval effort was very successful.

The Navy presence was not missed by reporters. In an attempt to satisfy the media, because of their questions about the Navy ships with underwater search equipment and the decontamination personnel in Palomares, the third official U.S. press release from Spain was made:

> Elements of the U.S. Navy and the U.S. Army are assisting Spanish authorities and the U.S. Air Force in the search for wreckage of the B-52 and KC-135 aircraft which suffered an accident during a refueling operation January 17.

Air Force officials reconfirmed that radiological surveys have found no indication of danger to public health or safety as a result of the accident.[29]

A restatement of the "no comment" policy came from the Department of Defense on 25 January, which also named the releasing agency in Spain:

> There should be no news releases or public statements of any kind on this subject without prior approval from Assistant Secretary Defense, Public Affairs (ASD[PA]). Before granting approval, ASD(PA) is coordinating with other military and defense agencies, the State Department and the U.S. Ambassador in Spain. In virtually all cases, releases will emanate from Embassy, Madrid after proper coordination with Government of Spain (GOS).[30]

The Aircraft Accident Investigation Board's Findings

At Palomares, the Air Force's Aircraft Accident Investigation Board (AAIB) gathered eyewitness statements, reconstructed the path of flight of the aircraft and the probable contact area, and collected all available facts concerning the cause of the accident. The structures and aerodynamics group of the board even required a crane to turn the wreckage so that fire pattern areas, structural failure points, and the like could be detected. The first formal board meeting was held on 20 January in a building in the village. The board was assisted and advised by a team from SAC; Air Force Deputy Inspector General for Safety; Air Force Oklahoma City Air Matériel Area; the Boeing Company; Eighth Air Force; and Second Air Force. Interviews were conducted in Palomares, Vera, Aquilas, Cuevas, and as far away as Murcia, Spain. An interpreter was required because the witnesses were Spanish fishermen, farmers, and shepherds who could not speak English.

On 28 January, the board returned to Torrejon to continue formal proceedings, interview surviving crew members, and complete the investigation. The report was forwarded to the 16th Air Force by 8 February.

The basic problem in the search for the #4 bomb was, as we at Sandia knew, to analyze the bomb ballistic trajectories and to define the search areas. The Aircraft Accident Investigation Board theorized that the B-52

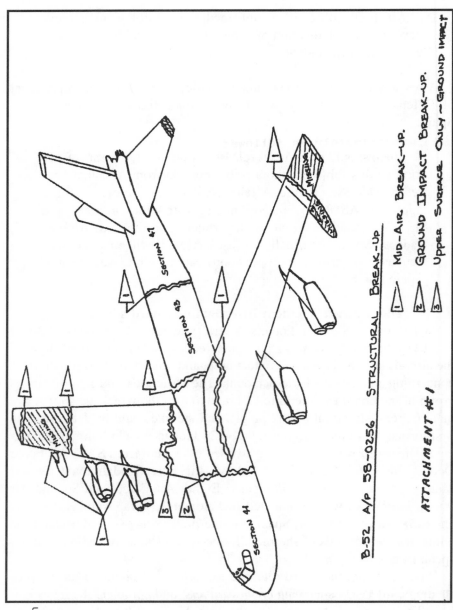

The Aircraft Accident Investigation Board's sketch of the B-52 breakup.

CERTIFICATE OF DAMAGE

KC-135A 61-273 and B-52G 580256 were totally destroyed as a result of major aircraft accident which occurred in the Saddle Rock Refueling Area, Spain. Total cost is approximately as follows:

KC-135A	$3,435,538
B-52G	$7.692,513
ADM 20C 60-612	$ 325,000
ADM 20C 60-701	$ 325,000
ADM 20C 60-736	$ 325,000
ADM 20C 60-778	$ 325,000
TOTAL	$12,428,051

George N. Payne

GEORGE N. PAYNE
Colonel, USAF
President, 16AF Accident
Investigation Board

The AAIB's cost analysis of the accident.

and all weapons experienced deceleration as a result of the breakup of the aircraft. The tail cover assembly from the #4 bomb was found northeast of the B-52 tail area and in line with the #2 and #3 bombs. After the initial B-52/KC-135 collision, a rupture of one longeron (the spine of the fuselage) occurred just aft of the B-52 fuselage/wing trailing edge juncture. The forward fuselage pitched downward and the high G loads snapped off the left wing. The weapons were then tossed out.

The #2 bomb was found with a major piece of the bomb rack still attached. It was theorized that high G loading had occurred, which caused the relatively massive weapons to separate at approximately four to five seconds after the longeron failure. It was reasonably certain that the #2 bomb was tumbling when it fell.

Bombs #1 and #3 apparently did not tumble, and they initiated parachute deployment in the first few seconds after release. Bomb #1's parachute was intact when the bomb was found.

Bombs #2 and #3 experienced a high-explosive detonation.

The main effort of the personnel at Camp Wilson was directed toward locating the missing weapon, sensitive documents, and equipment. The search, directed by Colonel Leland C. "Shep" Shepard, 16th Air Force, started from beyond the last known wreckage and worked toward the sea. Personnel were lined up abreast of each other, under the direction of three search leaders equipped with portable non-tactical radio units. A relay point for the radios was located on top of a small peak near the command post. Search areas were laid out each day and instructions given to the personnel as to what type of equipment they were to look for. Maintenance personnel and aircraft investigation and disaster control teams were involved in the search, along with other personnel, so that anything spotted could be duly noted, identified, and reported to the Intelligence specialists for plotting on maps.

During the first week, there were no adequate maps on which to plot the data from each day's search. Existing maps from Spanish sources proved to be inaccurate and did not even show the village of Palomares. On 24 January, the first of the mosaics prepared from the USAF aerial reconnaissance of 18 January arrived, and plotting of wreckage impact points and search areas was started. As photo mosaics became available, search areas were carefully defined and coverage could be more accurately determined without duplication of effort.

Studies of the aircraft track, wreckage pattern, locations of the three weapons, and the prevailing winds at the time of the accident indicated certain areas that should be searched for possible location of parts of the #4 bomb.

Chapter 4

The Systems Analysis Team's Results

We reconstructed where the accident occurred in the sky . . . by doing reverse trajectory calculations. . . . These calculations of the sky crash location all fell within a one-mile circle.

N THURSDAY, 28 JANUARY, General Wilson requested that I travel to Palomares to provide on-site help.[31] William Hoagland, a Sandian who was in Palomares aiding in the nuclear safety aspects of the accident, had recommended that individuals with the appropriate technical background from Sandia and the Air Force be assembled to make this system study.

Before flying to Madrid, I scrambled at the office on the 29th to pack my briefcase with the necessary materials to do aerodynamic calculations at Camp Wilson. A friend, Bob Peurifoy (who later became Sandia vice president of weapons and is one of the nation's experts on nuclear weapon safety), dropped by my office and presented me with a forked stick, like those used by "water witches" to identify underground water sites, to take to Spain to locate the missing bomb.

On arrival at the SAC Torrejon Air Force Base, I was immediately surrounded by several colonels asking detailed questions about the workings of the B28 bomb; the staff was certainly eager for information. Within an hour I boarded a T-39 Sabreliner jet, along with a Navy civilian consultant on underwater recovery, to fly the 235 miles from Madrid to San Javier and the Spanish Air Force Academy on the Mediterranean coast. The T-39 pilots looked about 15 years old, and frankly, I was a little concerned — though unnecessarily so — about their navigation methods and skills. The weather happened to be bad with clouds to 30,000 feet or so, and thus the young pilots flew far enough to ensure that they were over the Mediterranean before they let down. We broke through the overcast and then they turned and headed toward the land mass. I could see them carefully looking in all directions to obtain a land navigation check. We soon landed safely at San Javier.

An Army Huey helicopter then transported me the 117 miles to Palomares. This flight provided me with a good view of the rolling hills and the many trenches left intact from the Spanish Civil War, which brought back memories of Hemingway's *For Whom the Bell Tolls.* I arrived at the beach in the late afternoon, exhausted from the flight from Albuquerque, and was immediately questioned by several senior Air Force officers about the probable location of the missing bomb.

The other members of the Systems Analysis Team — Dick Bachman, an aircraft structural specialist from Wright-Patterson AFB, Ohio, and Martin Bennett and Dan Campbell, aeroballisticians from Eglin AFB, Florida — arrived at Palomares on 30 January, and we started reconstructing the accident from the testimony of the surviving airmen and the location of the aircraft and bomb debris.

Forty senior military officers (including General Wilson) and civilian personnel stayed at the Maricielo, a seaside motel, which was close to Garrucha. A woman named Anita and her 14-year-old nephew Marcos had remained at the Maricielo as the winter caretakers, but were ready to close down the lodgings and take a few weeks' holiday in Madrid. However, Angel Corujedo, a 66-year-old veteran of the Spanish Civil War who had lived in America and now accompanied General Wilson to interpret and intercede with the local Spanish officials and others on the General's behalf, persuaded the Maricielo's owner, Lieutenant General Rafael Cavanillas (who had been commander of Corujedo's unit in the war), to keep the motel open.[32] Anita and Marcos cooked and served meals, tended bar, cleaned, and made beds from the day of the accident until the Americans departed 80 days or so later.

The rooms were clean and adequate, though they were unheated and there was no hot water for shaving or showers. We persuaded Marcos to serve breakfasts of oranges, toasted bread, and coffee. We ate lunch at the open-air GI mess at Camp Wilson, but returned to the motel for leisurely dinners, typically offered from 9 p.m. until 12 a.m. Anita and Marcos prepared the many excellent courses of soups, fish, and veal, and each guest was somehow expected to order and drink a bottle of wine (and we obliged). The quarters and food at the motel were infinitely better than the tent quarters and the GI food at Camp Wilson.

After getting down to business, we of the Systems Analysis Team concluded that the B-52 tail probably rotated up when Major Messinger chopped the engine power; the KC-135 pilot probably increased power at the same time to correct the overrun, which would have rotated the KC-135 tail down, thereby decreasing the vertical distance separating the two aircraft. The 14-foot refueling boom probably struck the upper left longeron (the spine) of the B-52. The longerons are impact-sensitive because they are always in tension due to the large lift upload of the wings and the smaller negative lift download on the horizontal stabilizers. The damaged B-52 nose and left wing then pitched down. The left wing snapped off, creating a six- to seven-G up-force on the fuselage, which caused failure of the bomb rack holding the clip of four nuclear bombs. The fuselage also failed between the bomb-bay sections and separated.

The four bombs then separated from the rack at approximately 28,000 feet, four or five seconds after the longeron failed.

We reconstructed where the accident occurred in the sky (about two miles west of the shore) by doing reverse trajectory calculations, using the impact points of the three B28s and the B-52 engines. These calculations of the sky crash location all fell within a one-mile circle. The center of that accident circle was used as the starting point for our trajectory calculations for the #4 bomb.

We requested information on the wind direction and magnitude at the time of the accident. The 16th Air Force obtained some very sketchy meteorological data from weather stations at Gibraltar and Palma de Mallorca that indicated that the wind at the crash altitude was from 305 degrees at 60 to 75 knots (compared with the KC-135 navigator's estimate of 110 knots). Their estimated wind at 15,000 feet altitude was 45 knots from 270 degrees. In addition, no one knew whether or when the 16-foot or the 64-foot parachutes of the weapons opened. This large uncertainty in the wind and the parachute deployment made it impossible to accurately calculate the impact location of the #4 bomb.

A "figure of merit" that aerodynamicists use to compare the effect of winds on trajectories is the ground-impact velocity. The calculated impact velocity for the parachuting crew members was about 23 feet per second, which compares closely with the impact velocity of about 28 feet per second for the B28 with a 64-foot parachute deployed. The impact velocity for the B28 with a 16-foot parachute deployed was about 135 feet per second. Bombs #1 through #3, with impact velocities of 135 to 390 feet per second, were less affected by the wind and landed on the shore.

Major Messinger had opened his parachute immediately and drifted about eight miles out to sea. Captain Wendorf and Lieutenant Rooney had opened their parachutes at lower altitudes — around 15,000 feet — and landed about two miles out at sea. Captain Buchanan managed to open his damaged parachute just before impact and landed on the shore near the three bombs. Thus, the wind was a critical variable that we had to try to determine in order to calculate the trajectory of the #4 bomb.

A useful clue was that part of the tail plate (which holds the parachute system in the bomb) of the #4 bomb was found on the beach; this indicated that one or both of the parachutes may have been deployed.

Our uncertainty about winds and the 64-foot parachute deployment resulted in recommending a large sea search area (about eight square

Francisco Simo Orts, the fisherman from Aguilas who observed the #4 bomb enter the sea.
W. R. Barton

miles), code-named *Bravo*, that represented 90 percent of the calculated trajectory impact points. At the same time, we recognized that these trajectory calculations were not accurate and should not be used as the *primary* basis for a sea search.

We Systems Analysis Team members were discouraged because we could not define a small sea search area. However, after a few days, Captain Joe Ramirez, an Air Force attorney who was helping with the accident investigation, stopped by our tent at Camp Wilson and suggested that we interview fisherman Francisco Simo Orts. Joe had previously interviewed Simo and was convinced that he had seen the #4 bomb enter the sea close to his fishing boat.

On 3 February, we drove to the fishing city of Aguilas, where Orts lived and harbored his two boats, *Manuela Orts* and *Alfonso Orts*. We interviewed him in the mayor's office with Captain Ramirez as the interpreter.

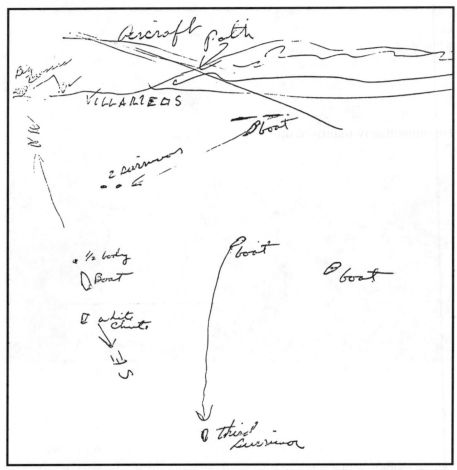

Simo Orts's sketch of locations of fishing boats, crew survivors, and "half a man" and white parachute that landed near his boat.

Simo indicated that he was fishing about five miles offshore when the accident occurred. He saw two parachutes enter the water close to his boat. The first, a small brownish one, carried what he described as "half a man, with the insides trailing" and splashed down about 25 yards away from his boat toward the shore. The second, a large white or grayish one, carried what he called a "dead man." The big chute floated down for six to eight minutes and sank immediately about 75 yards seaward from his boat. Simo indicated that this parachute was much larger than the orange and white parachutes of the B-52 crew members. I asked Simo to sketch the position of his boat and the objects he saw. I drew sketches of the 64-foot solid-canopy parachute and the 16-foot ribbon parachute. He immediately improved upon my sketch of the larger chute. He indicated the big chute was a solid-cloth canopy and was swinging considerably as it descended. In fact, solid-canopy parachutes oscillate about 30 degrees in terminal descent, whereas ribbon parachutes only oscillate about 3 degrees.

Simo's sketches of the two parachutes that landed near his fishing boat and a rough map of locations of the B-52 survivors and rescue boats certainly added veracity to his story. I was sure that Simo had seen the bomb case — the "dead man" — enter the sea with the 64-foot parachute deployed because of his description of its size and its large oscillations.[33] The "half man" was obviously the deployment bag of the 64-foot parachute, with the packing lines dangling, suspended by the 16-foot ribbon parachute. The parachute system worked as designed: the 16-foot chute

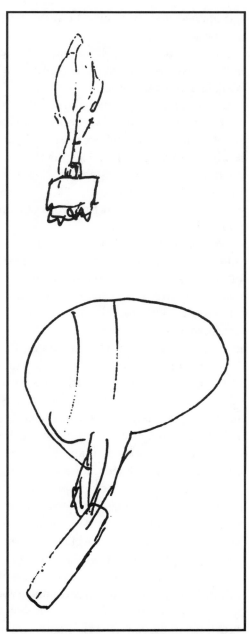

Simo Orts's sketch of 16-foot-diameter and 64-foot-diameter parachutes descending near his fishing boat.

had opened and then pulled out the 64-foot chute, which decelerated the B28 bomb.

After the interview, Simo and the mayor insisted on taking us to dinner at their favorite restaurant in Aguilas, where we dined on the best bouillabaisse I've ever tasted.

Simo was the most successful fisherman in the area — as evidenced by the fact that he owned two boats — because he could accurately navigate to the shrimp banks, where the sea floor dropped off rapidly to 2,000-foot depths. He navigated by "seaman's eye" by lining up known landmarks (such as smelter smokestacks, villages, ports, etc.) on the shoreline. Simo took U.S. Navy personnel back to the same location, five miles offshore, several times in the next few weeks to verify that he could accurately navigate using landmarks.

We concluded that Simo had seen the #4 bomb case enter the sea five miles offshore, but we could not be certain that the bomb was intact. We felt that it was possible that there could have been an in-air collision of the bomb with aircraft debris, which could have resulted in a high-explosive detonation. Then, the heavier primary of the nuclear weapon might have separated from the bomb case. Ballistic calculations indicated that the heavy primary would have landed on the shore near Palomares.

We documented the results of our studies, and the other members of the SAT requested that I give briefings of the results to General Wilson and Admiral Guest. We briefed General Wilson on the morning of 5 February and recommended that the sea search be centered on Simo's sighting. However, even though our trajectory calculations added credibility to what Simo had seen, the calculations alone were not sufficiently accurate to closely define a sea search area.

I had developed a good rapport with General Wilson shortly after arriving in Palomares because we discovered, during conversation, that we had both flown B-29 missions to Japan during World War II in the 20th Air Force. He had been an airplane commander based in Tinian, and I had been a navigator based on Saipan. This shared combat experience in the U.S. Army Air Forces did more to establish my credibility with him than did my college degrees in aeronautical engineering or being manager of the Sandia Aerodynamics Department that had helped design the B28 parachute system. General Wilson was very appreciative of our studies and arranged for us to brief Admiral Guest on his flagship, the 18,240-ton guided-missiles cruiser USS *Boston.*

In the afternoon, Navy personnel picked up the General and his staff and our Systems Analysis Team group in a small boat and took us out to the *Boston* for the briefing of Admiral Guest. As we were piped on board his flagship in a rather formal manner, the Admiral was waiting on the deck to greet us. I was carrying some large briefing charts, and as I climbed to the deck, the Admiral barked to one of his junior officers to carry these. Admiral Guest was somewhat rigid in his attitude and expected both the attendant civilian and military personnel to conduct themselves likewise. General Wilson, on the other hand, was much more informal in his approach to civilians and military personnel, although he left no doubt who was running the operation on the beach at Palomares. He exerted such strong control that it was almost like martial law at Camp Wilson and the village.

The briefing went fairly well, even though it was obvious that the Admiral didn't place much faith in the sighting or navigation skills of Simo the fisherman. He mentioned several times that he might start his search based on the sophisticated ballistic computer calculations of Sandia and the Air Force. But each time, I indicated that those calculations were made by our SAT group and that they were not particularly accurate; instead, we recommended that he start the sea search at the place where Simo Orts had seen the large parachute land.

The Systems Analysis Team group flew by helicopter to San Javier and on to Madrid by Air Force aircraft on 8 February. General Wilson arranged for us to stay for two nights at the Torrejon Air Force Base plush VIP quarters, which included a well-stocked bar. The General kindly asked his secretary to give us the VIP treatment as well. I requested the use of the SAC hotline to call my boss, Alan Pope, in Albuquerque, and Alan was on the line in a matter of seconds — this quick-response SAC hotline really impressed me.

The next day we were escorted through the Prado, and I was amazed at the collection of paintings by Rubens, Raphael, Goya, El Greco, Veláz-quez, and many other masters. Unfortunately, the museum was poorly lighted and the paintings were not well exhibited. We had an excellent dinner at Botins, one of Ernest Hemingway's favorite restaurants in old

Madrid, adjacent to the University of Madrid, one of the oldest universities in Europe. Botins was decorated with many colorful student banners, and we were serenaded by strolling musicians. The waiter indicated that they had been serving roast pig and roast lamb nightly at Botins for several hundred years. After dinner, we visited a nightclub to watch flamenco dancers. We enjoyed the R and R in Madrid, then returned to the United States on 11 February.

At the request of General Wilson, Sandia conducted drop tests at White Sands Missile Range in New Mexico on 15 February to determine the size and shape of a ground crater caused by impact of a part of the missing weapon. Sandians William Caudle and Gordo Miller conducted this project with the support of Kirtland Air Force Base.

William R. Barton from the Sandia Aerodynamics Department; Sam Moore, Sandia weapons engineer; and Paul Schneider, Albuquerque AEC representative, conducted additional system studies at Palomares from 16 February to 4 March. They had located a Palomares pharmacist and his assistant (named Rodrigez) who had observed, from different vantage points on the shore, a large parachute descending into the sea. The plots from these sightings intersected the Simo sighting area. Results of an intensive ground search and additional trajectory calculations indicated that the bomb was probably intact when it landed in the water. Bill Barton briefed General Wilson on 28 February and Admiral Guest on 1 March, recommending that the ground search be concluded and the sea search be centered around Simo's sighting. The team also briefed Jack Howard and Navy, Air Force, State Department, and AEC staff at the Pentagon on 8 March.[34] This briefing was repeated at SAC Headquarters, in Omaha, on the 9th, for General Ryan and his staff.

The Press

On 3 February, the first briefing for the media was held in Madrid; however, records of the recovery story indicate that the 16th Air Force public relations personnel were not present. Spanish Ambassador Duke told newsmen that 67 objects had been recovered from the sea, none of which had been identified as the missing nuclear device, and that the purpose of the recovery operation — to leave Spain as it was before — would continue until the job was done. Duke also announced that John Lindberg of Ocean Systems, who would work with the deep-sea recovery portion of the project, had arrived; that the submersible *Alvin* would be placed into service about 8 February; and that the submersible *Aluminaut* would arrive about the 17th. He also told reporters that authority for the release of unclassified photographs had been requested.

It was by then over two weeks since the accident, and the Department of Defense requested a comprehensive report from the 16th Air Force on the public affairs activities — namely, reactions of the press to the "no comment" policy, the degree of relationship with the Spaniards, and problem areas.

In reviewing the situation, the 16th Air Force indicated that there was high press interest: by that time, 54 newsmen, representing seven countries, had made 101 visits to the Palomares press office. In addition, many other reporters visited the area but did not officially contact the press center, and representatives of 23 media from six countries had made queries at Torrejon.

The reaction to the news ban was generally hostile, with "indignation, turning later to frustration." After all, the reporters were under pressure from their editors to produce stories. They thus turned to interviewing the local Spanish and Americans at the scene, which only led to "speculation and outright fabrication." To their credit, there was little difficulty with the Spanish press, since their reporting was usually factual. They, in fact, decried the sensationalism of some stories that had appeared in the French and Italian papers.

The 16th Air Force indicated to the Department of Defense on 5 February that they expected problems with the press in the future because of their experience with it over the last 17 days:

> We believe there will be increasing pressure for information on naval activities, particularly on the undersea research vehicle operation. It is anticipated that the press will strive to keep the story alive, and in the absence of official comment, may begin to speculate on such areas as water contamination, etc. Decontamination of crops continues to be an area of concern; however, the GOS coordinator is making every effort to dispel any false fears on this. We believe that Navy-furnished photography on their operations could reduce considerable pressure on the advanced camp and dispel many rumors.[35]

Sensationalism, however, seemed to thrive in the European headlines, and the Communist press especially featured very slanted, negative stories about U.S. nuclear bombers flying over Europe and the dangers of radiation at Palomares. Initially, following the accident, typical headlines erroneously referred to the weapon as an A-bomb:

U.S. Admits Downed B-52 Had A-Device (20 January 1966)

"Safe" A-Bomb Missing in Spain Plane Crash (21 January)

Contamination Reported at Air Crash in Spain (22 January)

Sonar Find Spurs Hunt for A-Bomb in Sea off Spain (24 January)

Silence Veils A-Crash Finds (24 January)

Bomber Crash Stirs Radioactive Scare (24 January)

Spanish Fear A-Bomber Crash May Have Damaged Crops (25 January)

Subs Reported Going to A-Hunt Site (28 January)

Spain Bars Atom Flights as U.S. Hunts Bomb (29 January)

A-Bomb Loss Will Peril Right to Other Bases (30 January)

Secrecy Shrouds Urgent Hunt for Missing A-Weapon (31 January)

Madrid Police Disperse Mob at U.S. Embassy (5 February)[36]

Colonel Donald C. Foster was sent from Washington to Torrejon and then to Palomares to study the problem. He discussed the situation with the Joint U.S. Military Advisory Group, Embassy, 16th Air Force, and Navy personnel and reviewed the newspaper stories. The consensus, diplomatic and military, was that immediate positive action is required to reverse the damaging news stories which have been, and are continuing to be, published worldwide. . . .

That a joint press briefing be held no later than 16 February at either Torrejon Air Base or preferably, if communications difficulties can be overcome, Palomares. On that occasion we should release a Defense Atomic Support Agency prepared paper on radiation hazards and should confirm the fact that we are searching for a nuclear weapon. . . .

That Commanders, Sixteenth AF and TF-65, be authorized to release, on a continuing basis, unclassified photography of their operation.

That Commanders, Sixteenth AF and TF-65, be authorized to provide routine briefings and land and sea press tours of the decontamination and search areas. However, the sea tours would be confined to light Landing Craft Vehicle Personnel or similar vessels.

That U.S. Embassy, Madrid, Sixteenth AF, and TF-65 establish an on-site ad hoc public affairs working group to make appropriate recommendations as dictated by subsequent events.[37]

As a result of this revised press policy, the fourth United States news release from Spain was issued on 2 March:

Search is being pressed off the Spanish Coast for the recovery of material carried by the two planes involved in the recent air collision and for fragments of wreckage which might furnish clues to the cause of the accident. Included aboard the B-52 which collided with the KC-135 tanker were several unarmed nuclear weapons, one of which has not yet been recovered.

When this search and investigation have been concluded further announcement will be made of the results.

The impact of the weapons on land resulted in a scattering of some plutonium (Pu 239) and uranium (U235) in the immediate vicinity of the point of impact. There was no nuclear explosion.

Built-in safeguards, perfected through years of extensive

safety testing, have allowed the United States to handle, store and transport nuclear weapons for more than two decades without a nuclear detonation. Thorough safety rules and practices also have been developed for dealing with any weapon accident which might result in the spilling of nuclear materials.

Radiological surveys of the Palomares area and its human and animal population have included detailed laboratory studies by leading Spanish and U.S. scientists through the 44 days since the accident. They have obtained no evidence of a health hazard. These experts say there is no hazard from eating vegetables marketed from this area, from eating the meat or fish or drinking the milk of animals.

Steps have been taken to insure that the affected areas are thoroughly cleaned up, and some soil and vegetation are being removed.

These measures are part of a comprehensive program to eliminate the chance of hazard, to set at rest unfounded fears, and thus to restore normal life and livelihood to the people of Palomares.[38]

Recommendation to Stop the Ground Search

The ground search of the disaster area was one of the most comprehensive activities of the Broken Arrow operation, with two high-probability areas designated for primary search: one approximately four square miles and the other two square miles. Search leaders were briefed each night on the area to be covered the next day.

By 2 March, the search areas had been covered in "fingertip to fingertip" line abreast formation, both longitudinally and laterally, an average of five times, and in some cases as many as nine times. As new information became available, new areas were identified and searched. Each night at approximately 1730, the search teams would return with bits and pieces of aircraft wreckage that had been overlooked. However, nothing was recovered that indicated that the #4 bomb had landed intact or that its high explosives had detonated and scattered bomb pieces over the area. Each piece was examined nightly by the Los Alamos and Sandia Corporation personnel, and all pieces were identified as aircraft debris or equipment.

On 3 March, after intensive ground search of the entire area and thorough investigation and elimination of 232 soil depressions, mine shafts, wells, and reservoirs, a message was sent by General Wilson to General John D. Ryan recommending termination of the ground search. The message was coordinated and agreed to by members of the Atomic Energy Commission and Sandia Corporation.

The testimony of fishermen, including Simo Orts, who were witnesses to the accident and who reported seeing a 64-foot white parachute descend and sink into the sea, left no doubt in the minds of the team and members of the search organization that termination of the ground search was in order. On 9 March, a message from General Ryan, Commander in Chief, SAC, to General John P. McConnell, Chief of Staff, U.S. Air Force, concurred with General Wilson's recommendation that the ground search be terminated. On 10 March, General McConnell made the same recommendation to the Assistant to the Secretary of Defense (Atomic Energy), with the provision that the capability to restart a land search be maintained as long as there was a potential need for same.

Chapter 5

The Plutonium Cleanup

. . .℞*adiation surveys were necessary to determine the extent of contamination and to provide a basis for definition of the decontamination operation.*

*A*T THE SAME TIME that the intense ground search for the missing nuclear weapon was being conducted — and indeed, well past the cessation of the ground search — the surveying for radiation and the decontamination of soil and plants was going on. After the first three bombs had been found, weapon #1 was lifted by helicopter and loaded on a truck, and debris from #2 and #3 were collected by Explosive Ordnance Disposal personnel and boxed for shipment. Heavy debris could not be lifted by helicopter at Sites 2 and 3 because downdrafts caused by the craft's rotors would cause the spread of contamination. The packaged debris was trucked from Palomares to San Javier and flown to Torrejon on 20 January. There it was repacked, minimizing the opening of the temporary containers. Before the shipment was airlifted to Amarillo, Texas, it was used at Torrejon as a calibration source for an aircraft-mounted radiation detection system. The shipment left Spain on 30 January.

Radiation monitoring in the village of Palomares, in conjunction with Spanish Junta de Energia Nuclear (JEN — Nuclear Energy Commission) personnel, was begun on 24 January. This consisted initially of monitoring the houses and random monitoring of the crops. By 3 February, however, it was established that a pattern of contamination ran through the village and connected Sites 2 and 3, thus making one complete pattern.

Radiation measurements were made on radial lines from the two craters until the readings were less than 1,000 CPM. Another method consisted of taking six to twelve radiation readings in each field and then averaging the readings. This average figure was placed on a sketch, as no maps were available at that time. In final form, this appeared as a rather random plot of the contamination; however, it proved to be a practical approach when the decontamination started. The initial surveys were never completely redone. Additional definition of the contaminated area was carried out later by monitoring and flagging isolines of 7,000 CPM (and above) and 700 CPM (and above) to conform to limits established during negotiations with the Spanish JEN. These isolines were transferred to maps of the area. On 30 and 31 January, a zero contamination line around the entire surveyed area was defined and staked with red flags.

Another contaminated area was located north of the village of Villaricos, approximately 4,000 feet from the eastern boundary of Site 3. This area was approximately three-quarters of a square mile. Contamination levels were low; the maximum was 7,000 CPM and most levels were less than 500 CPM. Because this area was isolated, rocky, and contained no cropland, it was not considered as a critical area for decontamination. The area was monitored jointly with JEN representatives and was believed to have been contaminated from Bomb #3, with prevailing weather at the time causing the break in the pattern.

These radiation surveys were necessary to determine the extent of contamination and to provide a basis for definition of the decontamination operation. Terrain surveying was a continuing program during the operation. It required many man-hours of work, from surveying relatively easy to very rough terrain. In the end, final surveys were performed on all decontaminated land before these properties were turned back to their owners; it was a difficult job performed under trying circumstances.

A hazard control line was impractical. The politics of the situation negated establishment of strict area control procedures and the placing of "contaminated area" signs. But the low levels of contamination in most of the pattern did not make this necessary.

Control points at the two areas of major activity, #2 and #3 craters, were established. Monitoring of personnel was routine, and by 24 January a 500-gallon water trailer was in use at Site 3 for decontamination of personnel and equipment. By the 27th, a similar unit was available for Site 2; however, by that time major recovery actions at that location were complete. In the interim, decontamination was done by means of buckets and bags of water, brushes, and soap.

A shower was installed at Camp Wilson on 25 January. This proved to be a great asset in personnel decontamination. On 3 February, a similar unit was set up at Site 3 for use by personnel working in the contaminated areas. Personnel involved in cleanup operations were issued protective clothing — gloves, anti-contamination coveralls, surgical masks, and surgical hats and boots — according to standard procedures covering the various cleanup operations.

The atmosphere was continuously sampled to determine the significance of airborne contamination. Particular attention was paid to those operations that generated dust. However, re-suspension of the plutonium was negligible.

Urine sampling of personnel was begun within three days of the accident. The initial samples were 24-hour volumes, but it was found that this was not practical, as it required personnel to carry the sample containers into contaminated areas (a logical reason for the high levels in some of the

Environmental and Biological Samples, Palomares **17 January-7 April 1966**	
Type	**Number**
Personal	
Urine	1,370
Nasal swabs	109
Film badges	22
Air	439
Water	
Locally tested	75
Sent to RHL	22
Soil	43
Vegetation	
Beans, cabbages, etc.	28
Tomatoes	74

initial samples). This function was later given to the camp medics to handle on a routine basis.

Initial results from the Radiological Health Laboratory (RHL) were encouraging, except for a few individuals who had apparently received extremely high-body burdens (high levels of contamination). These cases, however, subsequently proved to be contaminated samples. Repeat sampling indicated that no person received any significant body burden.

JEN officials handled a program of urine sampling for Spanish civilians; initial samples were collected on 30 Spanish personnel by U.S. staff. Primary emphasis was placed from the beginning on urine samples as an indicator of personnel exposure. Other techniques included some nasal swabs and an early use of film badges, which were sent to Wright-Patterson AFB for evaluation. To further control personnel radiation exposure and to ensure that no contamination had been carried into the base camp, the camp was monitored daily.

Elimination of contamination on personnel and clothing was awkward

Level of Contamination for All Areas	
1. Within zero line	630 acres initially 650 acres after winds occurred
2. Within 700 CPM line	500 acres
3. Above 700 CPM line	47 acres
4. Between 7,000 CPM and 60,000 CPM lines	41.5 acres
5. 60,000 to over 100,000 CPM	5.5 acres

and difficult during the early stages of the operation, but personnel show-ers were in use on 25 January and a laundry was installed on the 31st. Proper decontamination of coveralls became possible on 1 February. Many personnel came to camp with only limited clothing because they had been told they would stay for only a few days. Of course, develop-ments proved this to be an extremely conservative estimate.

If contamination was found on the skin during personnel monitoring, individuals were instructed to wash the contamination off and be re-mon-itored. If contamination was found on clothing, they were directed to change immediately and to wash the contaminated apparel. Supervisors were drilled on the necessity of complying with these instructions, and all personnel were likewise informed of their importance. At later stages, more exact precautions were possible, such as issuance of work clothes at each control point and then removal at the end of the day. These clothes were monitored before being re-worn.

Guidelines Established to Control the Hazards

Negotiations on levels and methods of decontamination proved a diffi-cult task, for there were different opinions on what was acceptable. The Spanish government had not established criteria for permissible levels, which was completely understandable because plutonium-producing facil-ities and nuclear weapons were nonexistent in Spain. Significantly, neither

Extent of Decontamination Operation

Soil removed:	1,088 cubic yards from 5.5 acres
Soil plowed: all cultivated land above 700 CPM	285 acres
Soil watered: (20 January-10 March)	285 acres
— water use:	100,000 gallons/day
Vegetation:	
— removed, mulched, stored (400 CPM or higher on vegetation)	400 cubic yards
— burned (less than 400 CPM on vegetation)	3,700 (2½ ton) truckloads
— all removed from areas where soil was above 700 CPM	285 acres

were there criteria in the United States for accident situations; the available criteria pertained only to plutonium processing plants and laboratories. There were, however, broad guidelines established from Nevada nuclear tests. A sense of urgency prevailed, primarily from a political standpoint, to arrive at criteria and begin the cleanup.

Dr. Wright Langham, probably the world's foremost authority on plutonium scattering in 1966,[39] and other representatives from the Atomic Energy Commission and the Los Alamos Scientific Laboratory recommended a method for handling the contaminated areas. Dr. Langham and the other AEC representatives decided, based on information summarized in the 1 May 1963 training manual of the Atomic Weapons Group, that the following procedures were adequate to control lifetime hazards associated with Sites 2 and 3:

1. All areas in which alpha counts per probe area are above 100,000 CPM will be removed to a depth of at least five to six cm and buried in an appropriate pit that will not permit seepage into the water table.

2. All areas with counts between 100,000 CPM and 7,000 CPM will have the present crops removed and buried. In all cases where the ground shows counts of 7,000 CPM to 100,000 CPM the soil will be sprinkled with water and plowed to a depth of at least 10 cm. After it is plowed, it will be sprinkled again and another monitoring survey conducted. Any spots that read above 7,000 CPM will be re-plowed and re-sprinkled until all readings are below the 7,000 CPM value.

3. All areas reading between 500 CPM and 7,000 CPM will be sprinkled with water to leach and fix the activity in the soil to minimize spreading by the wind. After sprinkling, the areas that read above 1,000 CPM will be re-sprinkled.[40]

This proposal was presented to the Spanish JEN for consideration. Although agreeing in principle with U.S. Air Force decontamination methods, the JEN did not agree on the levels at which various types of decontamination procedures would be taken. Several days of discussion and negotiations took place, and the following agreement was reached on 2 February:

1. Select a place with adequate conditions to build a disposal pit where highly contaminated soil and products will be deposited.

2. Build the pit with proper safety provisions for public health.

3. Annual vegetable crops with a reading above 200 CPM will be removed to the disposal pit, buried, and decomposed with quick lime.

4. Fruit orchards will be carefully water-washed to remove all contamination.

5. The ground areas treated as indicated in paragraphs 2 and 4 above will be re-monitored after completion of water-washing operation and depending upon the level found at that time, one of the following three procedures will be observed:

a. Soil above 7,000 CPM will be removed and deposited in the disposal pit. Soil will be replaced to the extent to which it was removed and re-fertilized.

b. Soil areas between 7,000 and 700 CPM shall be wet

down, plowed, and re-monitored for contamination. If the count does not come down to less than 700 CPM, the soil will be treated again until less than 700 CPM is reached.

   c. Soil areas below 700 CPM will be soaked with necessary water to bring contamination down to very low level and re-monitored for reading.

6. All monitoring will be done with the PAC-1S.[41]

It is significant to note that the cleanup criteria desired by the Spaniards was considerably more conservative than that recommended by Dr. Langham. The more stringent requirements were based on the Spaniards' fear of future complications resulting from the contamination.

During the period 3 February to 1 March 1966, the following changes and/or amendments were agreed upon by the JEN and the U.S. Air Force:

1. On 4 February 1966, agreement was reached with Eduardo Ramos, M.D., Chief Health Physicist for the JEN, that watering, following plowing, would not be a requirement. This decision was based on the fact that plowing followed by rototilling reduced the surface count to non-detectable readings.

2. On 8 February 1966, agreement was reached with [Dr.] Ramos . . . to permit hauling of harvested crops with a count of 200 CPM or less to the river bed for burning.

3. On 10 February 1966, agreement was reached with [Dr.] Ramos . . . to raise the level to 400 CPM for harvested crops which could be burned.

4. Changing attitudes on leaving the contamination in Spain resulted in negotiations being conducted by the U.S. Embassy and JUSM[A]G with their Spanish government counterparts during the week of 14 February 1966. There was considerable concern in both governments about leaving a "monument" to the accident in the form of a burial pit. These parties agreed that only soil with a surface contamination level of 60,000 CPM or greater would be removed from Spain. (Plowing an experimental tract of 0.09 acre — which had a surface count of 40,000 CPM — to a depth of eight inches followed by a second plowing to a depth of four inches demonstrated that this procedure

would maintain the surface contamination level at non-
detectable levels.)

5. On 24 February 1966, agreement was reached with Lt.
Colonel Santiago Norena (JEN) to permit burial of the previously scraped and piled soil in Area 2 (with a surface count
above 7,000 CPM but less than 60,000 CPM) in the pits that
had been dug for permanent burial.[42]

Difficulty was encountered in applying the original criteria to hilly,
rocky, uncultivated areas. The problem was resolved by a meeting at
Camp Wilson on 28 February 1966, which had in attendance Generals
Donovan and Wilson, Dr. Langham, Dr. Ramos, and other members of the
JEN and the U.S. Air Force. The following agreement was reached and
was the last of the amendments to the agreements on decontamination levels and methods:

1. Follow-up cleanup requirements in the uncultivated land
areas would be limited to Area 2. Earth would be removed
from:

a. Hot spots that showed counts of 60,000 CPM or above.
This earth would be included with that to be shipped from
Spain.

b. Land surface showing counts in excess of 10,000 CPM
would be washed, scarified, or dug up and raked.

c. Land surface showing surface counts of less than
10,000 CPM would be watered down where practical.

2. The permissible level of contamination was accepted as
10,000 CPM.

3. No work would be done in Area 6.[43]

The stated policy of the United States government was to decontami-
nate to levels that were more than adequate by U.S. safety standards. The
U.S. recognized that the Spanish government desired levels far beyond
safety requirements in the interest of combating psychological conse-
quences of the accident, but the chance that the decontamination levels
agreed to at Palomares would be pointed to as "safety standards" should a
subsequent contamination incident occur was a natural concern of U.S.
authorities. Even though safety standards for plutonium decontamination

exist, their employment in future incidents will probably be used as a talking paper for negotiations — a starting point to be overridden by psychological and political concerns.

Once the areas of contamination had been defined, removal of contaminated crops and soil started. Colonel Alton White, 16th Air Force, an agriculture graduate from Texas A&M who spoke fluent Spanish, directed these cleanup operations in coordination with the Spanish farmers. To keep track of the work, the contaminated areas were divided into plots following the outlines of the fields and gardens. The 844 plots covered 385.68 acres, with contamination readings from 0 to over 100,000 CPM. Within this area were demarcation lines for areas of less than 60,000 CPM where the soil was not removed. The soil in areas with contamination readings greater than 60,000 CPM was removed and shipped to the United States.

Vegetation was also marked, since vegetation with contamination readings under 400 CPM could be burned rather than removed. Eventually, 3,970 truckloads of vegetation were hauled from the area and destroyed. The remaining contaminated areas were leached by watering and washing down to reduce readings to as low a level as possible.

The crop removal activity started on 22 January, just five days after the accident; the plowing and scraping began on the 27th. By 10 February, the equipment in place to do this work included 16 water distributor trucks, 11 dump trucks, three road graders, two bulldozers, two front-end loaders (with two-cubic-yard buckets), five gang plows, five soil mulchers, and three tree-limb shredders. In a normal day of operation, 140 truckloads of crops were taken to either the burning area or the temporary storage site. The area for burning was at the dry riverbed near the impact point of the B-52 tail; this operation was done at night when winds were blowing out to sea. In late February, this area was moved closer to the shore, and a new road, which bypassed the inhabited areas, was completed from Site 3 to the beach.

Harvesting of the crops required considerable physical labor. Machetes were requisitioned from Gray Eagle supplies to cut tomatoes and other crops. And because the farmers had used cane poles to support the tomato vines, three tree-limb shredders were bought by SAC. The first arrived within 24 hours of the request, on 2 February. The cane poles were pulled from the ground, shredded, and the remains loaded into the trucks for delivery to the storage site.

Road graders were used for soil removal, where possible. The soil was moved into windrows and then into piles for loading on the trucks. But graders could not be used in the isolated hilly area around Site 2; this soil was removed by hand labor. When grader scraping left small hot spots (areas of high radiation concentration), plowing and/or hand removal was necessary. Scarifying the soil, with minimum turnover, dropped the radiation count to acceptable levels in the low contamination areas. This minimum movement of surface area was important at Site 2, where it was feared that major movement of topsoil in the fragile area would create a dust bowl.

Constant monitoring by the PAC-1S radiation detector was necessary to detect contamination spread, but in general, no problems were found. Occasionally a truck would turn up with positive readings and would require washing down. Operators of scrapers and plows were mostly unaffected, though personnel using shovels occasionally had some contamination on shoes, gloves, and outer clothing.

Washing of three buildings and some fences started on 30 January. Other buildings were washed, but in some cases this was not sufficient to lower the contamination level to the acceptable limit; whitewashing was then necessary. Rock-wall fences were also washed. Markers or walls of concrete block or tile were constructed to mark the land divisions where vegetation boundaries had been removed. Hot spots on irrigation ditch embankments were washed down to radiation levels below 500 CPM.

Site Analysis and Decontamination

The zero-count line surrounding the contaminated area at Site 2 was defined by 31 January, and the 7,000 CPM line, surrounding approximately 35 acres, had been marked by 2 February. Constant monitoring permitted establishment of the 100,000 CPM area by 10 February; it consisted of about four acres. Scraping of the soil and/or plowing was started on 1 February, and vegetation removal started on the next day. Although no one record exists of the number of truckloads hauled to the burial site, it was estimated to be approximately 400. About 470 truckloads of crops were hauled to the destruction site for burning. Use of water for washing down this area was difficult at first, because there was only a road to the crater area with no road through the contaminated area. Initially, a fire truck was used for washing, because the pumped stream would reach the desired distance. Later, regular water-distributing trucks with spray bars were used. As crops and soils were hauled away, the zero-contamination line was moved, and by 6 March all cane and vegetation, as well as the soil with over 60,000 CPM readings, had been removed.

At Site 3, located at the edge of the village of Palomares, the area with radiation over 7,000 CPM contained 11.5 acres of land, of which 10.5 acres were cultivated. The area over 100,000 CPM was established by 10 February as one and a half acres. Removal of crops started 22 January and was completed by 28 February; 2,815 truckloads were burned and 165 truckloads were sent to the disposal trench. Removal of the soil started about 1 February and was completed by the 5th. The first land was returned to the owners on the 7th.

Site 5, which was identified on 2 February, consisted of approximately nine and a half acres. The contamination level was not high and cleanup procedures were not as difficult. Crop removal was completed by 18 February; 402 truckloads were taken to the burning area. Plowing was done the following day, and by 24 February all land had been declared acceptable for use and returned to the owners.

The contamination spots at Site 6 were found on 4 February, and by the 16th, a zero line had been marked. Some question arose as to the origin of the radioactivity, and the U.S. Air Force asked that samples of the soil be sent to the AEC. Due to the rocky terrain and the sparse soil covering, machetes were used to shave off a layer of soil; usually less than half an inch could be removed. A total of 12 samples were taken with surface readings varying from 500 to 2,000 CPM.

Removing the Contamination

The soil with greater than 60,000 CPM and vegetation with greater than 400 CPM had to be removed from Spain, and although several methods were considered, it was decided to place the waste in 55-gallon barrels. On 23 February, the plan for removing the debris was firm enough that the Department of Defense summarized it as follows:

> Sixteenth Air Force has collected approximately 1,500 cubic yards of contaminated soil and vegetation for removal from Spain. This will satisfy removal criterion agreed to by Government of Spain. . . .
>
> Sixteenth Air Force proposed the use of oil drum-like containers. Number required is 5,500, and these have been con-

tracted for in Naples, Italy. CSAF has arranged with CNO for pickup of drums by the USS *Card* and delivery to Cartegena as soon as possible after production of drums is complete.

After filling, containers will be shipped to destination to be specified, but probably near Charleston, South Carolina, for rail shipment to, and disposal in, an AEC disposal area.[44]

It was planned to move the empty barrels with the USS *Alma Victory* and the USS *Cammon* and to use the USS *Boyce* to transport the filled barrels to the States. However, none of these ships could load at the temporary pier at the beach, and landing craft would be required to move the barrels to the ship. The *Alma* was ordered from Suez to Naples; she was loaded with the drums and sailed for Palomares on 9 March. The U.S. Army's 1418th Transportation Terminal Unit, Cadiz, Spain, was given the task of handling the barrels from ship to shore and back again. A Military Sea Transport Service representative was assigned to duty to assist this operation. The Navy had landing craft for use in shore-to-ship movement.

After these logistics preparations, the filling operation began. Sixty-five airmen were sent from Moron and Torrejon to augment the camp force — 12 carpenters, 3 welders, and 50 airmen to work at filling and handling the barrels.

Personnel manning the shovels wore respirator surgical masks, white coveralls, head coverings, and gloves. As each barrel was filled and covered, its sealing ring was affixed, the bolt tightened and welded in place, and two bands (placed at right angles) were spot-welded into place. Each was checked for contamination at approximately 72 points before it left the filling area. A flatbed transported the barrels to the beach, where radiation was spot-checked, then a roller conveyor system was used to move them to the ships.

When the *Alma Victory* arrived with its cargo of empty barrels on 11 March, 200 barrels that had been air-shipped to San Javier and trucked to Palomares were already filled and waiting on the beach. The *Boyce* arrived six days later to take away the filled barrels.

All work was completed by 24 March, and no radioactive contamination was detected during the entire operation.

The *Boyce* sailed on the 24th and arrived in Charleston on 5 April. Subsequently, the *Boyce* reported that inspection by AEC representatives indicated that the drums had arrived in satisfactory condition. Off-loading

General Delmar Wilson and Brigadier General Arturo Montel, senior Spanish officer at Camp Wilson, at the 29 March press conference regarding the last shipment of barrels of plutonium-contaminated earth to South Carolina. Camp Wilson is in the background.

from the *Boyce* was completed on 6 April, and loading the drums into railroad cars was completed on the next day. Twenty-six cars accompanied by two AEC couriers in the caboose departed Charleston on 8 April via Atlantic Coast Line Railroad and arrived at Dunbarton, South Carolina, the same day.

A summary of the contamination readings from the accident site was sent to the Atomic Energy Commission. None of the transport drums showed exterior contamination, but the radiation level of the material within varied from 0 to 300,000 CPM, with most of it at levels under 40,000 CPM. However, drums with soil that had come from an area of particularly high readings could not be identified because the moving process had mixed the barrels from various locations.

Two of the barrels were shipped to Los Alamos for Dr. Wright Langham to analyze, leaving 4,808 barrels for disposal in the trench grave prepared at the disposal site. The completion of this second phase of the disposal activity permitted 147 personnel from Camp Wilson to return to their home stations.

As the land at Palomares was cleared of contaminated soil, some of the topsoil was replaced with soil from the dry riverbed near the camp. As other areas were plowed and/or washed down to zero readings, the land was monitored by the U.S. Air Force and the Spanish Junta de Energia Nuclear, who agreed on its cleanliness and then turned it back to the owners.

Seven local tractors were rented for the plowing and harrowing of the new topsoil, and a local farmer was put in charge of the operation. Some complaints were made about the results, primarily that the land was not left in a uniform level condition. Thus, some of the land was reworked with the owners present; they remained on each plot until the job was completed.

By the evening of 1 April, all of the land within the contamination zone had been placed in the condition desired by the owners. All damaged culverts, irrigation ditches, bridges, and concrete block fences, which replaced some of the cactus fences that had been removed, had been replaced, painted, or repaired so that the countryside was returned to its original condition.

On file in the City Hall of Cuevas De Almanzora was a map showing the plots of the land. From this map, each area was identified, and a Certification of Decontamination Action was prepared to show the method of decontamination and the date. The certifcate was signed by both the JEN and the USAF representatives and was the unofficial record used as a file copy by the two agencies.

Another document was prepared that returned the land to the owners; this was signed by the JEN and U.S. Air Force representatives, the Spanish agronomist at the site, and Generals Wilson and Arturo Montel.

Spanish citizens filed 644 claims against the U.S. Air Force for fishing and farming losses and medical claims.[45] Total monies paid out for the 536 approved claims was $710,914.

Chapter 6

Recovered at Sea

What these accounts fail to take into consideration . . . is the immensity of the problem of locating the bomb. This operation met and overcame problems never before encountered in a sea search.

C OMMAND AND CONTROL WERE very important to the successful completion of the U.S. Navy's bomb recovery effort. Task Force 65 was a diverse assemblage of ships, naval personnel, and civilian specialists. As with any special purpose group brought together for a specific task, command and control assumed significant importance. The problems of command were also magnified by the political implications of this international incident.

Published accounts of Task Force 65 operations have noted that friction between some military and civilian personnel was detrimental to its mission. This friction is described as resulting from differences of opinion on the conduct of search operations and the importance of various findings. What these accounts fail to take into consideration, however, is the immensity of the problem of locating the bomb. This operation met and overcame problems never before encountered in a sea search.

Task Force 65 operated in a difficult environment and succeeded in its mission. All officers, seamen, and attached specialists of the force should be proud of this amazing feat — the recovery of a thermonuclear bomb 2,550 feet below the sea.

Communications, a vital component of command and control, were limited in the Palomares area. Two primary communications channels were required for the sea operations. One was local in nature and served the immediate operational requirements of the Task Force and its support units, but this system was unsatisfactory on many occasions.

Sufficient radio frequencies were unavailable to handle both administrative and tactical traffic because many ships were auxiliaries or Military Sea Transportation Service ships that were often limited in communications, personnel, and equipment and not fitted with a full military radio system. Included in the limited category was the ship-to-submersible circuit — the communications on the water's surface with the underwater vessels.

Communications to the submersibles *Alvin* and *Aluminaut* via the UQS-1 systems — underwater drones with hull-mounted search sonar towed by slow surface ships — were reliable, though the range capability was limited, and some interference was experienced when the two submersibles were operating in contiguous areas.

Even greater difficulty was encountered by the submersible *Cubmarine* and its control vessel, which was usually a minesweeper. Desired course information was generated from sonar contact with a pre-determined target and the submersible. The course to steer was then relayed to the open bridge by sound-powered phone, thence to the tending motor whaleboat by walkie-talkie radio, and finally to the *Cubmarine* by the Aqua Sonics underwater telephone. The resulting orders and information were often lacking in clarity and completeness.

The second communications channel of import was the one providing a reliable link between Admiral Guest and his immediate senior in the chain of command. This channel was not effectively established until the arrival of the USS *Boston* on 30 January 1966, which became Guest's headquarters until 15 March. It was through this ship's capabilities that the Admiral was able to request assistance and report progress to Admiral McDonald and the TAG in Washington, D.C.

Search Systems and Aids

Shipping assets required by the search and recovery operations grew from one fleet tug to a virtual armada of naval and commercial vessels. The urgency of the situation dictated that the initial contingent of Task Force 65 begin immediate action.

Little more than the basic facts concerning the aircraft accident were available to those early participants. The information available to Admiral Guest, upon his arrival at Camp Wilson on 24 January, consisted only of a rough estimate of the actual position of the collision, some guesses concerning the sequence of events following the breakup of the B-52, meager meteorological phenomena, and the location of the surviving crew members and assorted aircraft debris.

The sighting of an object suspended from a large white parachute, its position, and significance to the overall search effort were considered at an early date. On 21 January, before Admiral Guest's arrival, several actions had taken place that were to affect the entire search effort. The first two ships to arrive with any search capability, the minesweepers USS *Sagacity* and USS *Pinnacle,* started a random search that day in the area, using their hull-mounted search sonar. On the following day, the splash-down point of the large white parachute was confirmed when Spanish fisherman Simo Orts, who had been closest to the position in question on the day of the accident, was taken aboard the *Pinnacle.* Orts positioned the ship by seaman's eye — a visual reckoning.

A sonar search of the area resulted in two promising contacts at a depth of 2,040 feet. These contacts were reconfirmed by leaving the area and again asking the fisherman to position the ship over the splash-down point. Again the sonar contacts were obtained. Unfortunately, nothing further could be done toward identifying these contacts until a much later date.

It is rather ironic, if true, that Simo Orts attempted to pull on board his boat a very heavy object attached to a parachute. Unable to raise the weight and after having dented his boat in the attempt, he released the parachute and its hidden weight and watched it sink into the depths. How different the next 80 days might have been had he towed the object into shallow water — though this incident was not confirmed in official testimony.

To a world in the throes of a Cold War under the threat of nuclear conflict, security measures were high on the list of tasks assigned to Admiral Guest. Area surveillance was conducted by several sea and air units. Their mission was to ensure the integrity of the operational area and to maintain continuous surface and subsurface surveillance of the seaward approaches.

Surface units were selected from the ships assigned to Task Force 65, and air surveillance was provided by aircraft from nearby land bases. Perhaps the most significant surveillance and security operation was the tracking of the Soviet trawler *Lotsman* that observed the operation for 12 days. Area security was further enhanced by Spanish patrol craft that assisted in keeping the local fishing fleet from interfering with the search and recovery operations.

The random search effort begun upon the arrival of the *Pinnacle,* however, would have been a waste of time, men, machines, and money if it continued. Random search over such a large area — approximately 130 square miles — would have been inefficient and could provide no measure of search effectiveness.

Admiral Guest immediately designated specific search areas in alphanumeric order and assigned a priority to each, commensurate with the degree of reliability of the known facts and sightings. A number of factors were considered in determining the search areas: track of the B-52, wind direction and velocity from aircraft altitude to the surface, debris pattern ashore and near the beach, survivor splash-down points, Air Force and Sandia computer studies, sonar contacts, visual sightings from personnel on shore, and the observations of Simo Orts.

Alpha I was chosen by Admiral Guest as the highest priority search area. This selection was based on the mean of 11 Ocean-Bottom Scanning

Sonar (OBSS) and UQS-1 sonar contacts that were accorded high credibility because of the statements and plotted evidence from Simo Orts and the pharmacist and his assistant in Garrucha. Area *Alpha II* was selected as an extension of the debris pattern on the shore. Area *Bravo* was based on the Air Force and Sandia computer studies.

These area selections were not finalized until 17 February, by which time some 150 underwater contacts had been logged and many had been processed. The priorities finally assigned were designated by latitude and longitude and referenced to the then-available navigational charts of the area. However, these charts were not very accurate.

Neither were the navigational aids particularly accurate or suitable: radar for range and bearing fixes, Consolan (simple long-range aid providing position line over the North Atlantic), radio beacons, visual landmarks, and Loran-C (long-range aid that translated the time difference of reception of two pulse-type transmissions). Radar, Consolan, and radio beacons were not accurate enough for high-order positioning. Visual aids were not on a common datum base and in proper relationship to the search area; therefore, they were not useful in the search. And Loran-C was not suitable because of the distance to the transmitting stations, which resulted in weak signals in the search area.

The only medium- or large-scale chart covering the Palomares area, in the available charts for ships in the Mediterranean Sea, was H.O. 3930, with a scale of 1:233,640. This chart had been compiled in October 1935 from old Spanish charts; it would not be revised until October 1966, after the Palomares incident. The 1935 chart carried the note, "Some features on this chart may be displaced as much as one-half mile from their true position"; it was found that this was the rule rather than the exception.

One more chart existed, identified as SPN 108, covering the search area; it was reprinted by the Navy Oceanographic Office (NAVOCEANO) in January 1966 from a Spanish chart compiled in June 1960, from latest Spanish surveys. Inset on this chart were a chartlet of Palomares and Villaricos and a chartlet of Garrucha. Both of these chartlets were to a 1:25,000 scale, but neither the main chart nor the chartlets contained sufficient sounding data nor landmarks to be of value to AIRCRAFT SALVOPS MED.

The methods and evidence used to finally pinpoint the positions of the search areas varied widely. In addition to the need for a high-accuracy electronic positioning system, more accurate bathymetric (water depth) information was required. On a trip from Cartegena, the fleet ocean tug USS *Kiowa* transported to Palomares a complete Decca Hi-Fix navigation system, the Honeywell Sea Scanner and Precision Profiler, and underwater television cameras. The Decca Hi-Fix net, as installed, could only be used for relative positioning. This was remedied by employing a NAV-OCEANO geodetic survey team to fix the system transmitter locations on a common datum.

A support team was ordered into the area to operate the shore stations, since a large staff was required to maintain a Decca Net on a 24-hour basis. The navigation equipment was vital to Admiral Guest because he had discovered on arrival that there were no adequate sounding charts of the area.

The Decca system became operational on 6 February, but while it was being set up on a hill near Villaricos, the hydrographic ship USS *Dutton* started charting the ocean bottom. The initial bathymetric chart was delivered to the Admiral on 29 January, and the final bathymetric survey was completed on 26 February by the *Dutton.*

After the areas to be searched were determined, it was necessary to assign the search assets so that their capabilities and limitations matched the area requirements. It was soon recognized that additional search forces were needed for adequate in-shore coverage; this resulted in a request for more swimmers and divers.

The search plan that evolved was split into two components. One was the in-shore search area from the water's edge out to the 80-foot-depth contour line. This area was separated into block areas of a size that could be covered each day with a complete visual search, for 100 percent coverage, by the divers available.

The second component, the area outside the 80-foot depth, required more sophisticated methods. Because it was not practical to use divers for full coverage at the greater depths, such acoustic equipment as the Sea Scanner, the UQS-1, or the Ocean-Bottom Scanning Sonar were put into service. Divers were an integral part of the search team when the Sea Scanner was used; however, they were not part of the search team when the UQS-1 and OBSS were used, and thus identification and recovery teams were needed to follow up the contacts.

The selection of equipment for use in the various search areas was based on equipment characteristics, overall search results and the time required to cover a given area, and the ability of the available equipment to cope with the environments in the defined search areas. The prime source of contact data was sonar equipment. It detected items of all sizes and composition, from rocks and pebbles to large sections of the aircraft wings.

All contacts had to be identified either visually or photographically, because even the sonar with the highest definition (about six inches for the OBSS) was unable to provide sufficient data for acoustic identification. This dictated that all contacts be revisited and either sighted or photographed, which placed a major burden on the navigation systems available. In shallow water, over smooth terrain, results were satisfactory because ranges were short and inherent equipment errors were negligible. However, in water over 200 feet in depth, artificial light was required and range and bearing errors became significant regardless of the terrain.

The rough terrain in the southern half of *Alpha I* made acoustic systems totally ineffective. Towed search vehicles experienced the same difficulties. Inaccuracies in position increased with depth. Inability to detect the irregularity of the bottom in time to adjust the depth of the tow caused several collisions with the bottom that damaged sensors.

Towing duties were mainly assigned to the minesweepers, which experienced additional limitations in the form of tow speed and high winds and the loss of three towed vehicles. A difficult ship handling problem existed at the one- to two-knot tow speed of the Ocean-Bottom Scanning Sonar. This made the maintenance of a search track impossible in any increased wind or sea conditions. The physical requirements of recovery dictated diver assistance to shift the tow rig from astern to amidships boom for hoisting aboard, a relatively difficult and dangerous task in high seas.

Use of the underwater TV system required even more stringent operating limits. It could not be towed, and thus extremely accurate ship positioning was required for either search or contact identification. When a multipoint moor was feasible, search or identification could be conducted by a trial-and-error dipping procedure until the area accessible from that moor was covered. When a moor was not feasible, the operation was practically impossible.

The three general categories of search systems — with some overlap of capabilities — were divers, surface search systems, and submersibles.

Divers. During peak diver operations, approximately 125 Navy divers were assigned to the Task Force. Between 22 January and 7 March, they searched out, completely identified, and — when size permitted — recovered 143 aircraft debris contacts in an area covering three square miles. The swimmers and scuba divers were very effective and versatile.

Surface search systems. Although providing mission versatility and an improvement in depth capability over free divers, the hard-hat diver was less mobile because of the tether to the attending surface vessel. In addition, operating on the sea floor caused silt clouds that restricted his visibility and usefulness.

Three other surface-dependent systems were used by Task Force 65. The first, the underwater TV platform, was limited in depth capability, mobility and search rate, and required a moored vessel for control.

The second system, the Cable-Controlled Underwater Recovery Vehicle (CURV II), significantly enhanced search effectiveness. Although tethered to the mother ship, it combined sonar, closed-circuit television, cameras, and lighting with the ability to maneuver and recover relatively heavy objects from the ocean's floor to a depth of approximately 2,900 feet.

The third system, used by the oceanographic research ship USS *Mizar*, was one with a deep-water photographic capability — a sled towed on flat areas of the ocean floor, on which a transponder, a battery, one to four cameras, a sonar pinger, and two strobe lights were mounted. An underwater TV camera was available but not used on the sled. The *Mizar* was assigned to search operations in deep areas when it was not being used as a control ship for submersibles. It was primarily utilized for contact identification; a limitation, however, was the 10- to 24-hour time lag required to process the film. This time lag, inherent navigational error, and difficulty in maintaining a minimum fixed height above the bottom, as happened with the Ocean-Bottom Scanning Sonar, caused contact correlation errors and sometimes resulted in damage through collision with the bottom.

Admiral Swanson's Technical Advisory Group provided valuable technical guidance for Task Force 65 and arranged for special sea search capabilities to be sent to Palomares. On 19 February, the 3,300-ton *Mizar* arrived with the sonar, underwater television, and still cameras. She could survey one-quarter square mile daily, and her underwater tracking provided accurate readings as deep as 2,000 feet. The *Mizar*'s most important function, however, was to vector the submersibles *Alvin* and *Aluminaut* toward any object with which contact had been established. Guided by the *Mizar*, the submersibles could then attempt to attach a lifting line to the object and let the oceanographic ship hoist it to the surface on her main winch.

Submersibles. The submersibles were by far the most expensive, the most versatile, the most dangerous, and certainly the most glamorous of the recovery systems. Because they were research and development vehicles, they were without proven operating procedures. AIRCRAFT SALVOPS MED presented a fine opportunity to prove or disprove the system designs and to convince the world that future recovery operations would require comparable equipment.

Excluding swimmers and divers (for depth limitations), the submersible pilots, backed up by external cameras, represented the most reliable method of contact identification. Yet, in spite of this reliability, other factors posed problems. Time on the bottom was limited by crew fatigue, endurance of the life support system, and source of power for propulsion and illumination.

These manned systems required many more hours of maintenance time than their unmanned counterparts, and replacement parts were either difficult to obtain or nonexistent. A support organization or mother ship was required, thus increasing the personnel requirement severalfold. The vehicles were also limited to relatively good weather operations because of the launch and recovery requirements. In addition, they required a communications and navigation guide, while submerged, because they were not equipped with a self-contained navigation system. Once submerged, they had to depend on the sonar-derived steering instructions from the control ship to reach the general vicinity of the area in question.

Unless previously visited terrain features were recognized, each dive was an adventure into a new world with only general guidance by underwater telephone. The working ability of each submersible was limited by lack of leverage capability, making recovery of heavy objects difficult, if not impossible. Additionally, the danger of entrapment was always a possibility with rescue prospects doubtful.

Four submersibles were used during AIRCRAFT SALVOPS MED. The first on the scene, *Deep Jeep,* was also the first to be sent home. On station for only eight days, she made only one contact that was non-aircraft in nature. Disabled by a failure of one of her electric propulsion motors that was beyond the capability of the Task Force to repair, she was flown back to the United States. In summary, the *Deep Jeep* was characterized as an inadequate search vehicle with poor mobility, inadequate power, nar-

The USS *Albany* and the submersibles *Cubmarine, Alvin,* and *Aluminaut.*

The *Alvin* submersible, secured to the deck of the USS *Fort Snelling*, April 1966. *U.S. Navy*

LA BOMBA DE PALOMARES PARECE LOCALIZADA

Por fin, a los dos meses de incesante búsqueda, parece haber sido localizada por el submarino "Alvin", a unos mil metros de profundidad y a ocho kilómetros de la costa de Almería, la cuarta de las bombas H perdidas con ocasión del accidente aéreo registrado el 17 de enero sobre Palomares. Se dice que está envuelta en el paracaídas de que iba provista. La noticia no ha sido todavía confirmada en el campamento americano.

A 1966 photo of the *Alvin* by *ABC*, the largest newspaper in Madrid.

row field of view, difficult handling characteristics on the surface, poor maintainability, poor external lighting, no sonar, and a depth limitation of 2,000 feet.

On the other hand, the *Cubmarine* — the 22-foot-long, two-man visual search craft (with 14 portholes) developed by Perry Ocean Systems, Inc. — was extremely valuable. She spent 73 days on station and evaluated 44 contacts, 18 of which were aircraft debris. She arrived on 14 February, the day the *Alvin* and *Aluminaut* dived for the first time, and began diving on the next day. Although somewhat limited in endurance and depth capability (600 feet), which reduced her search effectiveness, the *Cubmarine* exhibited high mobility, good maintenance, and good coverage. Because of her limited utility, the manipulator was not used.

Next in size and best in maneuverability and adaptability to rugged terrain, the *Alvin* spent 72 days on station and evaluated six contacts, three of which originated from the B-52/KC-135 collision.[46] When compared to the *Cubmarine,* the *Alvin*'s contact results are misleading. Employed almost exclusively in deep water at the extreme limit of the predicted debris pattern, the *Alvin*'s opportunity for contact in either the search or identification mode was several orders of magnitude less than that of the *Cubmarine.* It is probable that the *Alvin* would have performed as well as the *Cubmarine,* given the same area assignment.

But the *Alvin* was not without her shortcomings. The limited endurance, about eight and a half hours, made searching large, flat areas inefficient. Normally eight hours of maintenance time between dives was required for battery charging and normal maintenance; this required dry docking in the well of the supporting Landing Ship Dock (LSD). The viewing ports were insufficient in both size and location, accentuating the need for an improved external lighting system. The *Alvin*'s installed manipulator arm had a working capacity of only 50 pounds, which limited the tasks that could be undertaken. The limited reserve buoyancy in the system provided practically no lift capability.

However, the *Alvin* was the most effective submersible for surveying the deep, narrow underwater canyons of *Alpha I.* She was highly maneuverable, 22 feet long with an eight-foot beam, and capable of operating to depths of 6,000 feet. She had a steel pressure sphere about seven feet in diameter made of high-strength steel 1⅓ inches thick. There was room in the sphere for a pilot and one or two observers, together with instrumentation and life-support equipment. The *Alvin* had four viewing ports to see ahead and behind the vehicle, and she cruised at two knots. Her equipment consisted of sonar, a ground detector, closed-circuit television, and a grappling arm. The *Alvin* was designed by Woods Hole Oceanographic Institution, and William O. Rainnie, Jr., an oceanographic engineer, was the chief pilot.

Largest of the submersibles — 51 feet long, 81 tons, and able to carry a crew of six — and designed for four times the endurance of the *Alvin,* the *Aluminaut,* developed and owned by Reynolds International, Inc., generally was not as effective for the tasks of search, identification, and recovery. Able to cruise at about four knots and dive to 15,000 feet, the bright orange *Aluminaut* amassed a record of 15 evaluated contacts, seven of which were aircraft debris. Although duplicating the *Alvin*'s 60 days of availability, and spending a comparable number of hours submerged, the *Aluminaut* amassed nearly twice the number of days lost to maintenance failures and in a standby status.

Several characteristics of the *Aluminaut* left room for improvement. Hull inspection and routine maintenance required the docking services of the LSD every four or five days. The *Aluminaut* was normally restricted from operating in rugged canyons and ravines because of her inability to readily avoid the terrain features and still operate within the short distances required by the prevailing visibility. Lack of an external photographic capability and a proven manipulator limited her identification and recovery usefulness.

It should be noted, however, that the *Aluminaut* did possess the lifting capacity to recover the lost nuclear weapon, but the operation was considered too great a risk to the vehicle and crew. Although carrying several types of equipment intended to provide a navigation capability, including underwater telephones, an electronic fathometer for depth measurements, scanning sonar, underwater lights, and underwater cameras, the *Aluminaut* was not able to determine its geographic position except by dead reckoning from the dive point. In an environment where visibility of 40 feet was the maximum, this navigation system was totally inadequate.

In the deep-water region in and about *Alpha I*, the *Alvin* and the *Aluminaut* were assigned visual searches in addition to contact investigation. This was due to the navigational limitations that prevented the submersibles from relocating sonar contacts that had been obtained by other means, and the generally unreliable nature of acoustic search in the rugged *Alpha I* bottom terrain.

Identification of contacts by acoustic means was impossible. Thus, all contacts not initially acquired either visually or by photograph required a revisit, either by diver, underwater TV, towed cameras, camera-equipped unmanned vehicles, or manned submersibles. All were useful and all contributed to the successful conclusion of AIRCRAFT SALVOPS MED.

One aspect of the operation affecting search or identification capability was subsurface navigation. The Decca Hi-Fix system could accurately position surface ships, but the relative position of submersibles could not accurately be tracked. Only the USS *Mizar* possessed an accurate tracking system, called Underwater Tracking Equipment. All other tracking systems were either grossly inaccurate or range-limited in determining where the search vehicle had been or where it was to go.

Search under any of the other tracking systems was essentially random. Some navigation capability was provided by bottom-planted transponders or pingers for use in conjunction with the vehicles' sonar; however, the profusion of frequencies and the loss of line-of-signal in rough sea-floor terrain severely handicapped these systems. The more sophisticated navigation systems installed in the *Aluminaut* were troubled with material deficiencies and were never operated satisfactorily.

Locating the Lost Bomb

On 1 March, 42 days after the accident over Palomares and on the tenth dive by the *Alvin,* a target, approximately 400 feet long rather than the expected 10, was discovered near the spot where Simo Orts had seen a parachute enter the ocean.

In short order, everyone would soon know that the discovery would lead to the missing nuclear weapon. Apparently, after water entry, the fourth bomb, still suspended from its parachute, descended to a depth of 355 fathoms (2,130 feet), riding the prevailing currents. It touched down on the rim of an underwater ridge and was apparently dragged over the edge by the current forces on the 64-foot-diameter parachute; it subsequently slid into the deep submarine canyon. From there it continued its descent to a depth of 425 fathoms (2,550 feet), leaving a smooth furrow. It was this furrow that was first found by the *Alvin* on 1 March while conducting contour searches at constant depth levels. Near the end of her submerged endurance, the *Alvin* attempted to follow the furrow down the steep slope but was unable to keep it in sight. Nearing the end of her battery life, she was forced to surface.

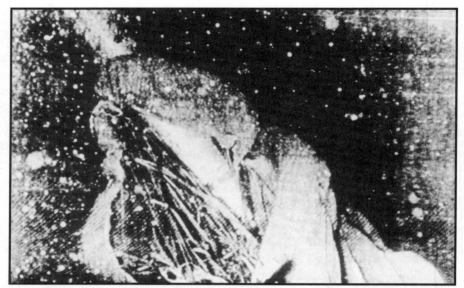

Underwater photo, 2,550-foot depth, of missing #4 bomb wrapped in 64-foot-diameter parachute.

Eight search missions in the same area and 12 days later, the *Alvin* relocated the furrow, but did not reach the end of the track because she was forced to surface, again due to battery exhaustion. The next day was spent in maintenance, and finally on 15 March the *Alvin* successfully backed down the furrow to discover a parachute-enshrouded object at a depth of 2,550 feet lying on a 70-degree slope. The first phase of the search was complete.

Flora Lewis, in *One of Our H-Bombs Is Missing,* documents conversation of the *Alvin*'s crew during the sighting:

> "This is *Alvin.* We have found a very large parachute. It appears to have some wreckage underneath it. I can't be sure exactly what it is. It's lying on a very, very steep gully. We can't get close enough to the chute to move it and see what's underneath. . . . However, part resembles a fin. . . ."
>
> "Echo this is *Alvin.*" This time there was calm triumph in the voice, no more strain or excitement. "How do you read me?"
>
> "I read you loud but not clear."

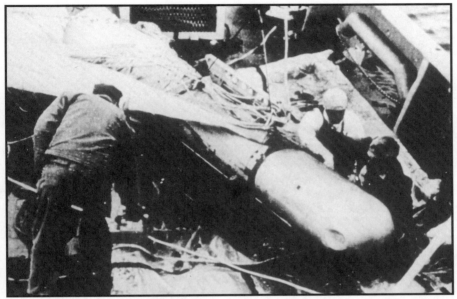

Recovered #4 bomb on the USS *Petrel*.

"I think we have enough identification. We'd like to skip clear of this area. There's several straps hanging down loose. There isn't any doubt in our minds about what we see. It's wrapped in the chute, but part of it shows. The thing is still lodged on a very steep slope. We got a good look at it. It's exactly the shape we've seen in the pictures."

"*Alvin.* This is an A-one job. Outstanding."

"Thank you."

The submarine was told to move to a position as close to the bomb as it could safely hold. It was to stay there and wait for the *Aluminaut* to come down as relief. That, too, would be a first. There had never before been a rendezvous of vessels in "inner space." While they waited the *Alvin* crew all began to talk at once, to the surface and to each other. The code was entirely forgotten.

"Did you see the bomb up there? We saw it. We got enough info. I don't want to get buttoned in there. I can see the nose of the bastard now."

Inspection of the #4 bomb aboard the USS *Petrel*. General Wilson is at the far left and Admiral Guest is leaning over the bomb.

"Yeah, I did too. No doubt in my mind."

"I don't know how we're going to salvage the bastard, do you? All we can do is roll it down the hill."

"That ain't a fin . . . that's part of the bomb-bay door or something."

"We'll have it pick it up by the chute."

"Yeah."

"It looks like a ghost down there now."

"I raised a big pile of muck with that move."

"You know, we were in a dangerous spot taking those pictures."

"I know it."

"I hope your cameras were working."

"Whaat!"

It was 11:35 a.m. when the *Alvin* first sighted the bomb, but by the time the *Aluminaut* got down and they were allowed to surface, it turned out to be their longest dive. They were submerged for ten hours and twenty-three minutes, almost the extreme limits of the little submarine's power, life-support system, and crew endurance.

To stay in place without using up all the *Alvin*'s power driving against current and drift, the pilots wedged the vessel in the mouth of a crevice, like a toothpick between two hunks of cheese. They sat in the dark waiting for eight hours, flicking on the lights from time to time but mostly with the lights off so as not to drain the batteries. When the black water at the south began to glow a brightening jade, it was a moment of almost as great excitement as finding the bomb.

What [Marvin] McCamis remembered most vividly about the whole day was the approach of the *Aluminaut.*

"It was beautiful, the most beautiful thing I ever saw. A great silvery-pink monster, it looked like, with great green phosphorescent eyes coming up silent through the water. I dreamed of seeing something like that, but I just thought it was a dream. I never thought I'd see it."[47]

The underwater photograph of the missing bomb was sent immediately to the Albuquerque Operations Office of the Atomic Energy Commission.

At the request of the AEC, I reviewed the photograph and positively identified the parachute and bomb system as a B28 and concluded that it must be the missing #4 bomb.

The Difficulty of Retrieval

During late February and early March, Pentagon officials had become concerned about questions from the Joint Congressional Committee on Atomic Energy. In particular, the officials needed to know what criteria should be used to make the decision to stop searching if the missing bomb wasn't found in a reasonable time. The United States could not afford to keep on looking indefinitely as the search was costing about $6 to $10 million a day. If the search was called off, it must be clear that every reasonable effort was made to locate and retrieve this highly classified bomb. There was always the outside possibility that the bomb might be retrieved from the sea by an unfriendly nation.

Hence, Cyrus Vance, Deputy Secretary of Defense, named a panel on 9 March to recommend if and when to stop the search. Members of this Search Evaluation Board consisted of Professor Robert Sproul, Cornell University (Chairman); Jack Howard, Assistant to the Secretary of Defense for Atomic Energy; Dr. M. Roy, Los Alamos Scientific Laboratory; Lieutenant General H. C. Donnelly, Commander, Defense Atomic Support Agency; Major General John B. McPherson, Office of the Joint Chiefs of Staff; Major General Andrew J. Kinney, Office of the Chief of Staff, USAF; Rear Admiral Leroy V. Swanson, Assistant Chief of Naval Operations; Scott George, State Department; and two representatives from the CIA. I was appointed as an alternate board member to Dr. Roy, who represented the AEC.

The only meeting of the Search Evaluation Board was held in Washington at the Pentagon on 15 March. Several briefings were given; I briefed the board on the System Analysis Team's (and Sandia's) analysis of the probable location of the missing bomb. But partway through the meeting, the board received the long-anticipated word that the bomb was located that day by the *Alvin* at 2,550 feet below the sea about five miles offshore. The board meeting was then concluded.

On 15 March, when the *Alvin* spotted what was considered to be the missing bomb, efforts were made to keep the matter quiet until positive identification could be made. Ambassador Duke instructed that the matter be handled with the "utmost secrecy" and that any announcements would be made by a publicity committee of Spanish and Embassy representatives. However, secrecy was not possible. Two days later the UPI filed a story from Frankfurt, Germany, stating the "officials were virtually certain the missing bomb had been located in the water and that a parachute for the weapon had been recovered." The Embassy decided to hold a press conference and announce the big event, and the State Department was notified.

But 15 minutes before the Embassy briefing of 18 March, word was received from the State Department that the briefing was canceled. Instead, a telegram from Secretary of State Dean Rusk was read to the reporters: "There have been hopeful developments but I cannot give you further information at this time. If we have a positive identification and recovery, we will so inform you."[48]

However, the next day, 19 March, the DoD and State Department approved the fifth news release from Spain, which was given by the military:

> With regard to the unidentified object and a parachute at a depth of some 2500 feet about four miles off the shore from Palomares, Rear Admiral William S. Guest, and Task Force Commander, has advised that because of the extremely steep slope off the sea bottom on which the object and parachute are resting, he proposed to attempt first to move them to a more favorable recovery area.
>
> If successful, this course of action will lessen the risk of having the object fall from its present precarious position into much deeper water. When the object is positively identified, an appropriate announcement will be made.[49]

The *Alvin* and the *Aluminaut* dived, whenever weather permitted, from 15 March until 19 March to set the stage for actual recovery. More hooks had to be driven into the gray canopy and more pingers and transponders installed to perfect a good tracking and navigational system.

The problem arose of how to lift the bomb and the parachute strapped to it from the narrow gully through the nearly 2,600 feet of water without tearing the lift lines and losing the weapon, perhaps for good, in one of the deep crevices at the bottom of the canyon. Task Force 65 thus designed and fabricated, in the workshop of the destroyer-tender USS *Cascade,* a rig called "Poodle" to aid in the recovery. It consisted of four long, pointed, spider-like steel legs that could sink firmly into the bottom's ooze. At the end of a 40-foot nylon line hanging from the Poodle was a 1,250-pound anchor designed to stabilize the contraption. From the anchor spread three 300-foot nylon lines equipped at the ends with grappling hooks. The idea was for the grappling hooks to bite into the parachute's canopy and thus provide an even-leverage hoist. Additionally, the Poodle had a camera and was festooned with electronic pingers and transponders tuned to the frequencies of the *Alvin* and the *Aluminaut.* The Poodle was both an underwater winch and a fixed navigational beam on which the two submersibles could home when needed.

Tad Szulc, in *The Bombs of Palomares,* details the failed attempt on 24 March to recover the #4 bomb:

> The immediate problem, of course, was to see to it that the bomb and parachute, now 2520 feet deep, would at least stay where they were. Just to get them back to their original ledge would be tantamount to getting them to what Guest had described as a "more favorable recovery area." But things were getting still tougher. Thirty-five-knot winds and heavy swells rose late on March 19 and continued on March 20, preventing new dives by the *Alvin* and the *Aluminaut.* The minesweeper USS *Salute* lost her towed vehicle carrying the ocean-bottom-scanning sonar. The fleet tug *Luiseno* parted her anchor cable. The oiler *Nespelen* lost her whaleboat. Admiral Guest became more taciturn than ever.
>
> For the next three days there was nothing for Guest to do except alternate his silences with curses addressed to the foul weather. From the afternoon of March 19 until the morning of March 23, a Wednesday, the Mediterranean mistral blew too hard to allow any search operations. All the men of Task Force 65 could do was wonder if the bomb was still where the *Alvin* had last seen her.
>
> On the morning of March 23 the *Alvin* prepared to dive, but a ballast-system problem delayed her a few hours. Finally she went down during the afternoon to begin one of the most nerve-racking episodes in the whole recovery operation. At first things went well. Rotating her mechanical arm, she succeeded

in placing two pingers and a transponder on the parachute. The bomb at least had stayed in the same place. Then the submersible pulled back to let the *Mizar* lower the Poodle anchor and a lift line about 80 feet from the parachute. The Poodle sat down on the slope, and the *Alvin* advanced again to grab one of its lift lines and try to hook it to the parachute. Then, inexplicably, the Poodle fell over on its side, its two other lines fouled, and there was nothing the *Alvin* could do to attach any of the three lines or to extricate the collapsed recovery contraption. In the end, the *Alvin* had to surface because her batteries were exhausted. Despite all the sophisticated tracking systems, the operation was still underwater blind man's bluff as far as the control crews on the surface were concerned.

The next day, Thursday, 24 March, there was no choice for Guest but to proceed with the recovery attempt. The *Alvin* dived again at noon and, despite poor visibility, immediately found the parachute. It promptly attached the Poodle's free line to at least six parachute risers. But at that point, probably owing to currents, the parachute began to billow and Guest concluded it would be extremely dangerous for the *Alvin* to remain any longer in the vicinity. In other words, the Admiral felt he could not risk the submersible and her crew in any further attempts to attach the Poodle's other lines to the parachute. He ordered the *Alvin* up and she surfaced at 7:30 p.m. The submersible's pilots reported that it was absolutely out of the question to untangle the Poodle's other lines and, as Guest put it later, "I had to make a decision to take the weapon." The only way to do it was to lift it on the single nylon line that the *Alvin* had succeeded in attaching to the canopy.

The lift was hooked to the *Mizar*'s winch, and at 8:00 p.m. the hoisting operation began. It was a clear, pleasant evening off Palomares, and the men were again optimistic that success might be just around the corner. The *Mizar*'s tracking system told Guest that the bomb and parachute had been lifted from the side of the gully into open water and that they were moving up along with the heavy Danforth anchor. The men held their breaths. For a full hour the nylon line was slowly reeled in on the *Mizar*'s winch. Then, at 9:15 p.m., the line took a sudden heavy strain and went awesomely slack. It had snapped, and the bomb with its parachute had dropped somewhere into the black depths of the Mediterranean canyons. Aboard the *Mizar* there were sudden silence and incredulity.[50]

The seventh news release was issued by Spain on the next day:

Admiral William S. Guest, Commander of Task Force 65, advises that operations for recovery of the object with attached parachute (previously located off the coast from Palomares, Spain) are proceeding satisfactorily. These operations must necessarily be accomplished slowly and cautiously due to the precarious position of the object on a steep submarine slope, and the great depth involved. At first weather conditions with high winds and choppy seas continued to periodically hamper current efforts. The limited endurance of the submersibles being employed and the necessity to recharge their batteries after each dive are primary factors which, with weather, control the tempo of our activities. Everything possible is being done to expedite recovery and identification of the object under these circumstances.[51]

This release from Madrid caused considerable unhappiness in Palomares, since it had been agreed that all such news items would be released simultaneously in Madrid and Palomares. General Wilson pointed out to General Donovan that fortunately the release had been a minor one; otherwise, the press at the scene would have been highly indignant. For a reporter at Palomares to utilize such a release, it would have been necessary to drive about half an hour to a phone and then struggle with the long-distance communications system of Spain. Wilson noted that the situation for the media was rough enough without antagonizing them further with advance releases in Madrid.

Indeed, the headlines in many European papers still cast a negative light on the U.S.:

Still Looking (7 February 1966)

Charges Near Catastrophe from U.S. Bomb: Soviets Say "Nuclear Volcano" in Sea off Spain (9 February)

Soviets Ask World Check on U.S. H-Bomb off Spain (19 February)

U.S. Faces Unending Cleanup Task (25 February)

Forty Days and Still No Bomb; U.S. Leaders Silent (27 February)

U.S. May Never Find Lost Bomb (27 February)

U.S. Reply to Moscow Charges Propaganda (27 February)

Spain Kept Lost Bomb Secret (3 March)

Air Crash Scattered Radioactive Fuel (3 March)

Deadly Clean-Up Task in 2 Areas (3 March)

U.S. Admits Loss of Nuclear Bomb (3 March)

Sun of Death Nearly Sets Coast Ablaze (date unknown)[52]

The next recovery phase started on 26 March. This search effort presented many of the same problems — and much anxiety — for the next eight days. On 2 April the object, still chute-enshrouded, was located on a bearing of 210 degrees true, a distance of 120 yards south from its position on 15 March, and now at a depth of 2,800 feet. The weapon did not again evade the searchers of Task Force 65.

The Cable-Controlled Underwater Recovery Vehicle, tethered to its 251-foot-long mother ship USS *Petrel*,[53] combined sonar, closed-circuit television, and cameras and lighting with the capability to maneuver and recover heavy objects from the ocean's floor. It was planned to use the CURV to attach three locally fabricated grapnels to the chute and its shroud lines. Each grapnel would have its own 5/8-inch nylon lift line.

One of the three grapnels was to be used as a "lazy tether" line, long enough to reach to the bottom of the deepest canyon in the area. But before this plan could be put into action, several tasks had to be accomplished. When the parachute-enshrouded object had been sighted on 15 March, the

CURV was modified to recover objects at a water depth of 2,800 feet. Because its design depth was 2,000 feet, some 900 feet of control cabling had to be spliced into position, a sea test had to be conducted off the coast of California, and then the vehicle had to be shipped to Palomares and installed on board the *Petrel*. Having demonstrated its ability to recover an object from a depth of 1,050 feet in the Palomares area, the CURV was ready to perform when the target was relocated on 2 April.

On 4 April, the CURV successfully attached the first grapnel to the apex of the chute. To this grapnel was attached 3,200 feet of 5/8-inch nylon line and an additional 1,500 feet of 3/4-inch nylon line on a buoy. On the 6th, a second grapnel was entangled in the chute shroud lines and connected to a second buoy by 5,000 feet of 5/8-inch nylon line. Subsequently, the *Alvin* reported that the weapon had moved some 300 feet down the slope, and thus the third grapnel was sent down on the CURV lest the weapon move below the depth capability of the vehicle.

While attempting to engage the third grapnel, the CURV became entangled in the parachute, and Admiral Guest decided to begin the second lift attempt. The two lift lines were engaged to the *Petrel*'s starboard amidships capstan through the starboard diving and boat booms so that both lines were hauled in simultaneously while the CURV's lines were tended over the stern. Taking up the slack on the apex line first, the two lines made the lift, and while the CURV lines were hauled in at the same time, care was taken not to put a strain on the parachute by that means. The action during the lift was recorded by the TV and cameras aboard the CURV.

When the weapon reached a depth of 50 feet and the top of the parachute was at the surface, divers transferred the load to a bridle extended from the ship's main boom. The long-lost nuclear weapon was swung aboard and gently lowered to a wooden cradle to await the rendering-safe procedures of the Explosive Ordnance Disposal team.

The nuclear bomb was hoisted aboard the USS *Petrel,* at 0840, 7 April, 80 days after the accident. A message of "Mission Accomplished" was transmitted to the Chief of Naval Operations.

The bomb was partially disassembled to accomplish the render-safe procedures and for ease of packing for subsequent shipping back to the States. Stewart Asselin, Sandia weapon designer, aided the Air Force and Navy ordnance experts in the render-safe procedures.

On 8 April, Admiral Guest briefed the press on the recovery in the stateroom of the USS *Albany,* his last flagship in Task Force 65. After the briefing, the *Petrel,* with the bomb on deck, sailed past the *Albany* at some 400 yards and then reversed engines and backed within 35 yards of the *Albany* so that the press could get a good view of the recovered H-bomb. Admiral Guest, General Wilson, General Montel, and others stood in a semicircle around the weapon during this first public display of a thermonuclear bomb.

The ninth and final new release from Spain was given to the press the day after the bomb was recovered:

> The fourth and final weapon from the January 17 crash near Palomares, Spain, has been recovered today and will be transported directly to the United States. The casing was intact. The weapon was located on March 15 in 2,500 feet of water, approximately five miles off shore by units of Task Force 65. Photographs taken at that time tentatively identified the object as the missing weapon. The recovery of this weapon brings to a close the search phase of the operation. No release of radioactivity into the coastal waters has occurred. All wreckage fragments and associated aircraft material of interest to the accident investigation have now been located and recovered.[54]

This officially ended the bomb story from Palomares.

A few days later, a joint communiqué prepared by the State Department, the Department of Defense, and the Atomic Energy Commission was issued to the military, Department of Energy, and State Department on guidance for publicity of nuclear weapons. This bulletin directed an immediate return to the previous policy — that is, nothing could be said about the nuclear bombs and no more pictures could be taken by the public.

As far as the Palomares bomb was concerned, all that could be said was that "the weapon will be delivered to a facility of the Atomic Energy Commission after it is returned to the U.S."

Epilogue

The Palomares accident became one of a growing number of close calls regarding nuclear detonation that were being carefully monitored by the weapon designers. . . . Palomares has become what American and Spanish scientists say is a living laboratory, the only civilian population to be exposed to a plutonium accident.

9 T TOOK 80 DAYS to locate and recover the Palomares missing nuclear bomb; the estimated cost was $50 to $80 million. About 4,000 on-site Air Force, Navy, Army, and civilian staff, plus several hundred personnel in the United States and Europe, participated in this operation. The accident resulted in adverse international publicity for the United States, primarily from the Soviet and other Communist press.

Sandia, the nuclear ordnance bomb designers, played a small but critical role in this cleanup and recovery operation,[55] though only six Sandia personnel were on-site during the 80 days, and then only for short periods of time. The real heroes of this operation were the Air Force and Navy personnel and Dr. Wright Langham of Los Alamos National Laboratories.

Air Force General Delmar Wilson and his 600-man team combed the land for weeks looking for the missing bomb, established the limits of the plutonium scattering from alpha radiation measurements, plowed up 285 acres of tomato fields and settled 536 claims for $710,914, and shipped more than 4,800 barrels of contaminated soil to North Carolina. Colonel Alton White did an excellent job in supervising these operations for General Wilson and working with the Spanish farmers. And Dr. Langham negotiated with the Spanish Junta de Energia Nuclear on the extent of the plutonium scattering and the required cleanup.

In the face of strong political pressure and many setbacks due to weather and equipment failure, Admiral William Guest demonstrated a bulldog tenacity and superb organizational skills in coordinating the recovery work of about 3,400 sailors and civilians. The crews of the *Alvin* and the *Aluminaut* risked their lives daily, diving into the narrow ravines, some 3,000 feet below the sea.

Francisco Simo Orts was awarded $10,000 for help in finding the #4 bomb; he had filed a claim for $5 million. (Ancient sea laws indicated that because he had seen the bomb enter the sea, he could claim it.) He was also reimbursed $4,566 for help in the recovery of the B-52 crew, damage to his boats and equipment, and use of his boats for several searches.

That the crash didn't cause a nuclear detonation was a reassurance to the designers at the national laboratories. However, the costs of this accident were still far too high.

As a result of the accident, overflying Spain with nuclear bombs immediately ceased at the request of the Spanish government.[56] In addition, the number of CHROME DOME flights was reduced.[57]

Secretary of Defense McNamara had become convinced that Strategic Air Command's airborne alert program was no longer necessary for U.S. national security, and in February 1966, taking advantage of the increased attention placed on nuclear weapons safety after the Palomares incident, McNamara proposed the complete elimination of the airborne alert program.

The Secretary raised three major arguments in favor of ending the operation. First, the Ballistic Missile Early Warning System was by then fully operational and had been improved with the addition of over-the-horizon radars. Bombers on ground-alert at bases in the United States therefore could be launched with sufficient confidence to make airborne alerts unnecessary. Second, the U.S. bomber force was no longer as significant a part of U.S. retaliatory capability; airborne bombers, McNamara told Congress, "provide us only a small capability, and it has become particularly small in relation to our huge and growing missile force."[58] Third, eliminating daily airborne alert operations could save over $123 million from the Pentagon budget.

The Joint Chiefs of Staff and the Strategic Air Command strongly objected to the elimination of the program, however, and questioned McNamara's analysis. They argued that, at a minimum, a small number of daily B-52 flights was needed to provide SAC with realistic training exercises. Supporters of the airborne alert also informed President Johnson, who maintained the authority to make the final decision, that the airborne alert flights would

> put a certain number of aircraft closer to target with more accurate delivery capability than the missile force . . . [and would] also further reduce the possibility of a surprise disarming attack against the United States.[59]

Eventually, a compromise between McNamara and the Joint Chiefs was reached, and SAC was authorized by the Secretary of Defense to continue only "whatever airborne alert was consistent with the regular (bomber crew) training program and would not require additional funds."[60] President Johnson then approved the curtailed program in June 1966, permitting SAC to maintain a significantly smaller force of only four nuclear-armed bombers on airborne alert each day.

The Palomares accident became one of a growing number of close calls regarding nuclear detonation that were being carefully monitored by the weapon designers — in particular by Stan Spray and Bill Stevens of the Sandia Nuclear Safety Department. (The 21 January 1968 Thule accident is discussed in Appendix A.) These accidents and incidents indicated that a new and different safety philosophy was critically needed.

Laboratory tests simulating the real accidents of fire, electrical shorts, mechanical crashes, and resulting high-explosive detonations demonstrated that the independence that had been assumed in the design of multiple safety devices did not always exist. Thus, in the late 1960s, Sandia Corporation started a major program to develop a new weapon safety philosophy.

Many designers believed that our aging stockpile of nuclear weapons was becoming unreliable. A few foresaw a pressing need to replace or upgrade the stockpiled weapons to eliminate the now-known deficiencies in safety, security, and control.

Advanced development studies had shown that brute-force approaches (overdesign in strength) could neither be depended upon in very severe accidents nor be accommodated in weight-sensitive modern weapon systems. Other advanced development studies had demonstrated that an approach that co-located critical firing components (designed to fail irreversibly above normal operating environments) along with extra-strong safety switches inside an exclusion volume held significant promise for enhanced nuclear safety. This strong-link/weak-link approach, combined with employing insensitive high explosives in the nuclear device (to minimize the probability of plutonium scattering), emerged as the most promising safety design philosophy.

With this knowledge, Herman Mauney of Sandia drafted a proposal that outlined the design for a new bomb to replace the B28.[61] In September 1971, this proposal received wide distribution in the Department of Defense and Atomic Energy Commission communities, and the concepts presented were ultimately incorporated into the Military Characteristics for new weapons.

Sandia's Bob Peurifoy added these concepts into a retrofit of the B61 bomb in 1973. The B61 became the first stockpiled weapon to use TATB (an insensitive high explosive originally developed during World War I) and the co-located critical components and strong safety switches in an exclusion volume in the bomb.

Thus, there was a positive nuclear safety outcome — albeit long-term

— from this expensive, unfortunate Palomares accident. Through the vig-
ilance and tenacity of foresighted Sandians and Lawrence Livermore and
Los Alamos staff, these troublesome and frightening accidents resulted in
a positive benefit: a safer design philosophy. This new safety philosophy
has since been incorporated into the U.S. nuclear stockpile.

In 1992, a summary of lessons learned from the Palomares accident was
given by U.S. Marine Corps Major R. W. Simmons, of the Interservice
Nuclear Weapons School:

> Politics drove the entire episode. Politics drove the USAF to
> adopt Operation Chrome Dome. The Soviets vehemently con-
> demned the U.S. throughout the entire process. The Soviet
> accusations ranged from dropping the weapons as an excuse to
> launch World War III, violating the Limited Test Ban Treaty,
> and claiming that large portions of the Mediterranean Sea had
> been contaminated by the weapons. Palomares and its conse-
> quences hardly dampened the intensity of the Cold War be-
> tween the two superpowers. The accident also affected the
> already scheduled 1968 basing right negotiations between the
> United States and Spain.
>
> Public affairs presented numerous challenges for both the
> media and the military. The Neither Confirm Nor Deny policy,
> even in 1966, did not stand up to the harsh scrutiny that the
> media will bring. The facts that the accident occurred on for-
> eign soil, that contamination had been released, and that a
> weapon had been lost further compounded the problem for the
> military public affairs' program. In addition, the United States
> had a cumbersome chain that had to be negotiated before any
> information could be released. The world media that covered
> the story had to contend with less than four star accommoda-
> tions and an extremely limited communications infrastructure
> while searching for their story.
>
> The United States learned a host of technology lessons.
> These ranged from the inadequacy of its radiacs for use in
> detecting radiation in the field, that radiac instruments would
> have to be repaired in the field instead of back at a major fixed
> installation, the U.S. Navy experimental submersibles really did
> work, and that the nuclear weapons had been designed proper-

ly because they did not go nuclear when involved in an accident.[62]

Finally, *The New York Times,* in a 28 December 1985 story, "Where H-Bombs Fell, Spaniards Still Worry," tells of a visit to Palomares almost 20 years after the accident:

> . . . Today, worried about the delayed effect of radiation in creating cancer, many of the villagers fear that the contamination of their bodies may become apparent soon.
>
> It is a fear heightened, they say, by nearly 20 years of being kept in the dark by the Spanish authorities.
>
> Feeling pressure from a growing political clamor, the Nuclear Energy Board only last month let the more than 500 villagers who had been studied see their medical reports for the first time. The board proclaimed that radiation danger was negligible.
>
> . . . Palomares, a mile off the coastal highway, is a collection of tidy, white-washed houses. The village got running water only last summer.
>
> Almost every yard sports tethered goats and plastic hothouses growing the strong-tasting local tomatoes, about the only crop that will survive. The region is so hardscrabble in places that "Lawrence of Arabia" was filmed nearby.
>
> Three bombs fell on the village, and a fourth, which took three months to find, fell into the sea. Their nuclear cores had not been activated, preventing explosions.
>
> But two of the bombs that hit land underwent "chemical explosions" on impact. That spread a light shower of plutonium that Francisco Mingot, a physicist with the Nuclear Energy Board, said "will last in the soil forever."
>
> . . . Bomb-grade plutonium is considered far more toxic than the uranium common in most nuclear reactors. Thus Palomares has become what American and Spanish scientists say is a living laboratory, the only civilian population to be exposed to a plutonium accident.
>
> . . . The Nuclear Energy Board has shuttled nearly 600 villagers to Madrid for intensive tests over the years. Only about

60 showed signs of contamination, and only one came close to exceeding international safety levels, Mr. Mingot said. He said someone would have to eat "millions of tomatoes" for them to be dangerous. "There is no risk," he said.[63]

The recovered B28 bomb cases #1 and #4 are on permanent display in the Sandia National Laboratories National Atomic Museum in Albuquerque, New Mexico.

For its "invaluable assistance" in locating the missing bomb, Sandia National Laboratories received letters of commendation from Secretary of Defense R. McNamara; Deputy Secretary of Defense Cyrus Vance; Chairman, U.S. Atomic Energy Commission, Dr. G. T. Seaborg; and U.S. Air Force Generals J. D. Ryan, H. T. Wheless, D. E. Wilson, and D. L. Crowson.

Appendix A

Nuclear Weapon
Accidents

Introduction

THE DEPARTMENT OF DEFENSE and Department of Energy compiled a list in December 1980 and January 1981 of all nuclear accidents involving U.S. weapons — 32 of them. *The Defense Monitor* published this list, along with comments by the Center for Defense Information (CDI). This Appendix, reproduced verbatim, details these 32 accidents and provides an excellent background history. It is included with this manuscript in order to place the Palomares incident in the right perspective and to provide the reader with an overall look at United States nuclear accidents. I have added, at the end, comments to this compilation where errors are believed to exist. All material in brackets is from the Center for Defense Information. Since 1980, no known accidents have occurred.

———— ⌣ ————

The Defense Monitor
1981 Center for Defense Information, Washington, DC
ISSN #0195-6450   Vol. X, No. 5

U.S. Nuclear Weapons Accidents: Danger in Our Midst
Defense Monitor in Brief
— The Department of Defense has reported 32 serious accidents involving U.S. nuclear weapons.

— The Pentagon reports provide interesting and disquieting information about the dangers of nuclear weapons accidents but are incomplete, uneven, and vague.

— Nuclear weapons are located at hundreds of places throughout the U.S. and in foreign countries and are transported frequently from place to place.

— Not all significant mishaps involving nuclear weapons and their components are reported under the current Department of Defense nuclear accident reporting system.

— As the numbers of nuclear weapons increase in the 1980s the risk of nuclear accidents will increase.

U.S. Department of Defense Nuclear Weapons Accidents 1950-1980
Introduction
Attached are unclassified summaries describing the circumstances sur-

rounding 32 accidents involving nuclear weapons. Also attached is the Department of Defense (DoD)/Department of Energy (DOE) definition of "accident" used in researching this project. Twenty-six of these summaries were first released by the Air Force in 1977; another was prepared following the Titan II explosion in Arkansas in September 1980. There never has been even a partial inadvertent United States nuclear detonation despite the very severe stresses imposed upon the weapons involved in these accidents. All "detonations" reported in the summaries involved conventional high explosives (HE) only. Only two accidents, those at Palomares and Thule, resulted in a widespread dispersal of nuclear materials.

Nuclear weapons are never carried on training flights. Most of the aircraft accidents represented here occurred during logistic/ferry missions or airborne alert flights by Strategic Air Command (SAC) aircraft. Airborne alert was terminated in 1968 because of:

— Accidents, particularly those at Palomares and Thule,
— The rising cost of maintaining a portion of the SAC bomber force constantly on airborne alert, and,
— The advent of a responsive and survivable intercontinental ballistic missile force which relieved the manned bomber force of a part of its more time-sensitive responsibilities. (A portion of the SAC force remains on nuclear ground alert.)

Since the location of a nuclear weapon is classified defense information, it is Department of Defense policy normally neither to confirm nor deny the presence of nuclear weapons at any specific place. In the case of an accident involving nuclear weapons, their presence may or may not be divulged at the time depending upon the possibility of public hazard or alarm. Therefore, in some of the events summarized here, the fact of the presence of nuclear weapons or materials may not have been confirmed at the time. Furthermore, due to diplomatic considerations, it is not possible to specify the location of the accidents that occurred overseas, except for Palomares and Thule.

Most of the weapon systems involved in these accidents are no longer in the active inventory. Those include the B-29, B-36, B-47, B-50, B-58, C-124, F-100 and P-5M aircraft, and the Minuteman I missile [BOMARC].

With some early models of nuclear weapons, it was standard procedure during most operations to keep a capsule of nuclear material separate from the weapon for safety purposes. While a weapon with the capsule removed did contain a quantity of natural (not enriched) uranium with an extremely low level of radioactivity, accidental detonation of the HE element would not cause a nuclear detonation or contamination. More modern designs incorporate improved redundant safety features to insure that a nuclear explosion does not occur as the result of an accident.

This list of accidents was compiled by DoD/DOE researchers during December 1980-January 1981. The researchers reviewed all available records of the military services and DOE, applying current definitions to determine if an event warranted categorization as an accident.

For example, one event not covered by these narratives was included in a "Chronology of Nuclear Accident Statements," released by DoD in 1968: "18 March 1963, Titan (I) Missile Burned in Silo near Moses Lake, Washington." The researchers found, however, that only a small retro-rocket on the missile had accidentally fired. The missile and its warhead were not damaged. That event does not warrant inclusion in a list of accidents involving nuclear weapons.

Another event from the 1968 list, involving a U.S. Navy Terrier missile (20 January 1966, NAS Mayport, Florida) was not considered to be an accident, but has been categorized as a significant incident. In that incident, a nuclear warhead separated from the missile, and fell about eight feet [aboard the USS *Luce,* a guided missile frigate. The event occurred on 19 January]. The warhead was dented; no other damage occurred.

The events outlined in the attached narratives involved operational weapons, nuclear materials, aircraft and/or missiles under control of the U.S. Air Force, U.S. Navy or a DOE predecessor agency, the Atomic Energy Commission. The U.S. Army has never experienced an event serious enough to warrant inclusion in a list of accidents involving nuclear weapons. The U.S. Marine Corps does not have custody of nuclear weapons in peacetime and has experienced no accidents or significant incidents involving them.

To the best of our knowledge, this list is complete. Reporting requirements varied among the Services, particularly in the earlier period covered by these narratives, so it is possible but not likely that an earlier accident has gone unreported here. All later events, however, have been evaluated and are included if they fall within the established definition of an accident.

Department of Defense Definition of an Accident

An "accident involving nuclear weapons" is defined as an unexpected event involving nuclear weapons or nuclear weapons components that results in any of the following:

— Accidental or unauthorized launching, firing, or use, by United States forces or supported allied forces, of a nuclear-capable weapon system which could create the risk of an outbreak of war.
— Nuclear detonation.
— Non-nuclear detonation or burning of a nuclear weapon or radioactive weapon component, including a fully assembled nuclear weapon, an unassembled nuclear weapon, or a radioactive nuclear weapon component.
— Radioactive contamination.
— Seizure, theft, or loss of a nuclear weapon or radioactive nuclear weapon component, including jettisoning.
— Public hazard, actual or implied.

U.S. Navy Definitions

NUCFLASH
Any accidental or unauthorized incident involving a possible detonation of a nuclear weapon by United States forces which could create the risk of nuclear war between the United States and the USSR.

BROKEN ARROW
a) The accidental or unauthorized detonation, or possible detonation of a nuclear weapon (other than war risk);
b) Non-nuclear detonation or burning of a nuclear weapon;
c) Radioactive contamination;
d) Seizure, theft, or loss of a nuclear weapon or component (including jettisoning);
e) Public hazard, actual or implied.

BENT SPEAR
Any nuclear weapons significant incidents other than nuclear weapon accidents or war risk detonations, actual or possible.

DULL SWORD   Any nuclear weapon incident other than significant incidents.

FADED GIANT   Any nuclear reactor or radiological accidents involving equipment used in connection with naval nuclear reactors or other naval nuclear energy devices while such equipment is under the custody of the Navy.[64]

Department of Defense Summaries of Accidents Involving United States Nuclear Weapons 1950-1980

No. 1, 13 February 1950 / B-36 / Pacific Ocean, off coast of British Columbia

The B-36 was enroute from Eielson Air Force Base [near Fairbanks, Alaska] to Carswell Air Force Base [Fort Worth, Texas] on a simulated combat profile mission. The weapon aboard the aircraft had a dummy capsule installed. After six hours of flight, the aircraft developed serious mechanical difficulties, making it necessary to shut down three engines. The aircraft was at 12,000 feet altitude. Icing conditions complicated the emergency and level flight could not be maintained. The aircraft headed out over the Pacific Ocean and dropped the weapon from 8,000 feet. A bright flash occurred on impact, followed by a sound and shock wave. Only the weapon's high explosive material detonated. The aircraft was then flown over Princess Royal Island where the crew bailed out. The aircraft wreckage was later found on Vancouver Island.

CDI: Sixteen crewmen and one passenger parachuted safely and were rescued. An accompanying B-36 flew safely to Carswell Air Force Base. No mention is made of an attempt to recover the nuclear weapon and presumably it is still in the ocean. As early as 1950 nuclear weapons were carried to and from Alaska. The B-36 was operational from 1948-1959 and 325 were built.

No. 2, 11 April 1950 / B-29 / Manzano Base, New Mexico

Aircraft departed Kirtland Air Force Base [Albuquerque, N.M.] at 9:38

p.m. and crashed into a mountain on Manzano Base approximately three minutes later killing the crew [of 13]. Detonators were installed in the bomb on board the aircraft. The bomb case was demolished and some high explosive (HE) material burned in the gasoline fire. Other pieces of unburned HE were scattered throughout the wreckage. Four spare detonators in their carrying case were recovered undamaged. There were no contamination or recovery problems. The recovered components of the weapon were returned to the Atomic Energy Commission. Both the weapon and the capsule of nuclear material were on board the aircraft but the capsule was not inserted for safety reasons. A nuclear detonation was not possible.

CDI: *The New York Times* reported the B-29 crashed in a "remote secret area of Sandia Special Weapons Base . . . and burned, shooting up flames visible for fifteen miles." Manzano Mountain was used as a "dead storage" site where outmoded weapons were stored. The B-29 was the United States' first nuclear delivery aircraft and comprised the majority of our strategic bomb force through 1952. The *Enola Gay* was a B-29 which dropped the bomb on Hiroshima. By June 1948 only 32 B-29s were modified to deliver nuclear weapons. All were assigned to the 509th Bomb Group. The B-29 was operational from 1943-1954; 3,970 were built.

No. 3, 13 July 1950 / B-50 / Lebanon, Ohio

The B-50 was on a training mission from Biggs Air Force Base, [El Paso,] Texas. The aircraft was flying at 7,000 feet on a clear day. Aircraft nosed down and flew into the ground killing four officers and 12 airmen. The high explosive portion of the weapon aboard detonated on impact. There was no nuclear capsule aboard the aircraft.

CDI: The explosion was heard over a radius of 25 miles and made a crater 25 feet deep and 200 feet square. The B-50 was an improved derivative of the B-29 with the same general appearance. It was operational from 1948-1953 and 370 were built.

No. 4, 5 August 1950 / B-29 / Fairfield-Suisun Air Force Base, [Fairfield,] California

A B-29 carrying a weapon, but no capsule, experienced two runaway propellers and landing gear retraction difficulties on takeoff from Fair-field-Suisun Air Force Base (now Travis Air Force Base). The aircraft attempted an emergency landing and crashed and burned. The fire was fought for 12-15 minutes before the weapon's high explosive material det-onated. Nineteen crew members and rescue personnel were killed in the crash and/or the resulting detonation, including General Travis.

CDI: The aircraft crashed near a trailer camp occupied by 200 service families. The explosion of 10-12,500 pounds' conventional explosive bombs shattered more than half of the 50 automobiles and trailers, blasted a crater 20 yards across and six feet deep and was felt 30 miles away. The fire could be seen for 65 miles. There were also 60 people hurt.

No. 5, 10 November 1950 / B-50 / Over water, outside United States

Because of an in-flight aircraft emergency, a weapon containing no cap-sule of nuclear material was jettisoned over water from an altitude of 10,500 feet. A high-explosive detonation was observed.

CDI: There is no record of recovery of this nuclear weapon.

No. 6, 10 March 1956 / B-47 / Mediterranean Sea

The aircraft was one of a flight of four scheduled for nonstop deploy-ment from MacDill Air Force Base [Tampa, Florida] to an overseas air base. Takeoff from MacDill and first refueling were normal. The second refueling point was over the Mediterranean Sea. In preparation for this, the flight penetrated solid cloud formation to descend to the refueling level of 14,000 feet. Base of the clouds was 14,500 feet and visibility was poor. The aircraft, carrying two nuclear capsules in carrying cases, never made contact with the tanker. An extensive search failed to locate any traces of the missing aircraft or crew. No weapons were aboard the aircraft, only two capsules of nuclear weapons material in carrying cases. A nuclear detonation was not possible.

CDI: This disappearance of the B-47, its crew, and nuclear weapons material was assumed to be an accident. The B-47 was America's first jet bomber and was operational from 1951-1965. Faster than its predecessors, it lacked the range to reach the Soviet Union from the U.S. and thus bases were established in England and French Morocco in 1950-51. Two-thousand and sixty B-47s were built.

No. 7, 27 July 1956 / B-47 / Overseas base

A B-47 aircraft with no weapons aboard was on a routine training mission making a touch-and-go landing when the aircraft suddenly went out of control and slid off the runway, crashing into a storage igloo containing several nuclear weapons. The bombs did not burn or detonate. There were no contamination or cleanup problems. The damaged weapons and components were returned to the Atomic Energy Commission. The weapons that were involved were in storage configuration. No capsules of nuclear materials were in the weapons or present in the building.

CDI: The crash occurred at Lakenheath Royal Air Force Station, 20 miles northeast of Cambridge, England. The plane was part of the 307th Bombardment Wing and had recently come from Lincoln Air Force Base, Nebraska. As part of what was called "Operation Reflex," B-47 bombers were regularly rotated, usually on a 90-day basis, to bases in the United Kingdom and North Africa. In the storage igloo were three Mark 6 nuclear bombs, each 12 feet long and six feet in diameter. Each bomb had about 8,000 pounds of TNT as part of its trigger mechanism. The blazing jet fuel did not ignite the TNT and was extinguished by the base fire fighters. The four crewmen were killed. "It is possible that a part of Eastern England would have become a desert" had the TNT exploded and showered radioactive materials over a wide area, said a now retired Air Force general who was in the United Kingdom at the time. "It was a combination of tremendous heroism, good fortune and the will of God," said a former Air Force officer who was on the scene.

It is not clear when American nuclear weapons were first deployed to Europe. The process went through several stages. In early July 1950 President Truman approved the stockpiling of non-nuclear components at forward bases in England. On 6 December 1950, President Truman endorsed the Joint Chiefs' request that non-nuclear components of atomic bombs be stocked on board the aircraft carrier, USS *Franklin Roosevelt,* stationed in the Mediterranean.

No. 8, 22 May 1957 / B-36 / Kirtland Air Force Base, New Mexico

The aircraft was ferrying a weapon from Biggs Air Force Base, Texas, to Kirtland Air Force Base. At 11:50 a.m. Mountain Standard Time, while approaching Kirtland at an altitude of 1,700 feet, the weapon dropped from the bomb bay taking the bomb bay doors with it. Weapon parachutes were deployed but apparently did not fully retard the fall because of the low altitude. The impact point was approximately 4.5 miles south of the Kirtland control tower and 0.3 miles west of the Sandia Base reservation. The high explosive material detonated, completely destroying the weapon and making a crater approximately 25 feet in diameter and 12 feet deep. Fragments and debris were scattered as far as one mile from the impact point. The release mechanism locking pin was being removed at the time of release. (It was standard procedure at that time that the locking pin be removed during takeoff and landing to allow for emergency jettison of the weapon if necessary.) Recovery and cleanup operations were conducted by Field Command, Armed Forces Special Weapons Project. Radiological survey of the area disclosed no radioactivity beyond the lip of the crater at which point the level was 0.5 milliroentgens. There were no health or safety problems. Both the weapon and capsule were on board the aircraft but the capsule was not inserted for safety reasons. A nuclear detonation was not possible.

CDI: In a *New York Times* report of the 1968 list of accidents, there is mention of a B-36 bomber dropping an atomic bomb near Kirtland Air Force Base in 1956 that was publicly reported. Either a similar event did occur in 1956 or it has been confused with this event.

Inadvertent Explosion

Nuclear weapons are designed with great care to explode only when deliberately armed and fired. Nevertheless, there is always a possibility that, as a result of accidental circumstances, an explosion will take place inadvertently. Although all conceivable precautions are taken to prevent them, such accidents might occur in areas where weapons are assembled and stored, during the course of loading and transportation on the ground, or when actually in the delivery vehicle, e.g., an airplane or a missile.   Atomic Energy Commission/Department of Defense
The Effects of Nuclear Weapons *1962*

───── ✈ ─────

No. 9, 28 July 1957 / C-124 / Atlantic Ocean

Two weapons were jettisoned from a C-124 aircraft on 28 July 1957 off the east coast of the United States. There were three weapons and one nuclear capsule aboard the aircraft at the time. Nuclear components were not installed in the weapons. The C-124 aircraft was enroute from Dover Air Force Base, Delaware, when a loss of power from number one and two engines was experienced. Maximum power was applied to the remaining engines; however, level flight could not be maintained. At this point, the decision was made to jettison cargo in the interest of safety of the aircraft and crew. The first weapon was jettisoned at 4,500 feet altitude. The second weapon was jettisoned at approximately 2,500 feet altitude. No detonation occurred from either weapon. Both weapons are presumed to have been damaged from impact with the ocean surface. Both weapons are presumed to have submerged almost instantly. The ocean varies in depth in the area of the jettisonings. The C-124 landed at an airfield in the vicinity of Atlantic City, New Jersey, with the remaining weapon and the nuclear capsule aboard. A search for the weapons or debris had negative results.

CDI: Three of the 32 accidents occurred while transporting nuclear weapons from one place to another, using the C-124 "Globemaster" transport. In this instance weapons and a nuclear capsule were being taken to Europe. The weapons were jettisoned within an area 100 miles southeast of the Naval Air Station, Pomona, N.J., where the aircraft landed. The two weapons are still presumably in the area, somewhere east of Rehobeth Beach, Delaware, Cape May and Wildwood, N.J. Plutonium-239, an isotope used to fuel atomic bombs, has a half-life of 24,400 years and remains poisonous for at least half a million years.

───── ✈ ─────

No. 10, 11 October 1957 / B-47 / Homestead Air Force Base, [Homestead,] Florida

The B-47 departed Homestead Air Force Base shortly after midnight on a deployment mission. Shortly after liftoff one of the aircraft's outrigger tires exploded. The aircraft crashed in an uninhabited area approximately 3,800 feet from the end of runway. The aircraft was carrying one weapon in ferry configuration in the bomb bay and one clear capsule in a carrying case in the crew compartment. The weapon was enveloped in flames which burned and smoldered for approximately four hours after which time it was cooled with water. Two low order high explosive detonations occurred during the burning. The nuclear capsule and its carrying case were recovered intact and only slightly damaged by heat. Approximately one-half of the weapon remained. All major components were damaged but were identifiable and accounted for.

CDI: Four crewmen were killed.

No. 11, 31 January 1958 / B-47 / Overseas base

A B-47 with one weapon in strike configuration was making a simulated takeoff during an exercise alert. When the aircraft reached approximately 30 knots on the runway, the left rear wheel casting failed. The tail struck the runway and a fuel tank ruptured. The aircraft caught fire and burned for seven hours. Firemen fought the fire for the allotted ten minutes' fire fighting time for high explosive contents of that weapon, then evacuated the area. The high explosive did not detonate, but there was some contamination in the immediate area of the crash. After the wreckage and the asphalt beneath it were removed and the runway washed down, contamination was detected. One fire truck and one fireman's clothing showed slight alpha contamination until washed. Following the accident exercise alerts were temporarily suspended and B-47 wheels were checked for defects.

CDI: The crash might have taken place at a U.S. air base in Sidi Slimane, French Morocco. An earlier Air Force document reported, "Contamination of the wreckage was high, but that of the surrounding area was low." The *New York Times* of 8 June 1960 mentions a nuclear weapons accident having occurred "at a United States field near Tripoli, Libya," but gives no date.

No. 12, 5 February 1958 / B-47 / Savannah River, Georgia

The B-47 was on a simulated combat mission that originated at Homestead Air Force Base, Florida. While near Savannah, Georgia, the B-47 had a mid-air collision at 3:30 a.m. with an F-86 aircraft. Following the collision the B-47 attempted three times to land at Hunter Air Force Base, Georgia, with a weapon aboard. Because of the condition of the aircraft, its airspeed could not be reduced enough to insure a safe landing. Therefore, the decision was made to jettison the weapon rather than expose Hunter Air Force Base to the possibility of a high explosive detonation. A nuclear detonation was not possible since the nuclear capsule was not aboard the aircraft. The weapon was jettisoned into the water several miles from the mouth of the Savannah River (Georgia) in Wassaw Sound off Tybee Beach. The precise weapon impact point is unknown. The weapon was dropped from an altitude of approximately 7,200 feet at an aircraft speed of 180-190 knots. No detonation occurred. After jettison the B-47 landed safely. A three square mile area was searched using a ship with divers and underwater demolition team technicians using Galvanic drag and hand-held sonar devices. The weapon was not found. The search was terminated 16 April 1958. The weapon was considered to be irretrievably lost.

CDI: Some accounts of nuclear weapons accidents list a 12 February 1958 accident involving a B-47 off Savannah, Georgia. An earlier DoD narrative was more precise on where it landed. "The best estimate," they say, "was determined to be 31 degrees 54' 15" North, 80 degrees 54' 54" West."

No. 13, 11 March 1958 / B-47 / Florence, South Carolina

On 11 March 1958, at 3:53 p.m. Eastern Standard Time, a B-47E departed Hunter Air Force Base, Georgia, as number three aircraft in a flight of four enroute to an overseas base. After level off at 15,000 feet, the aircraft accidentally jettisoned an unarmed nuclear weapon which impacted in a sparsely populated area six and one-half miles east of Florence, South Carolina. The bomb's high explosive material exploded on impact. The detonation caused property damage and several injuries on the ground. The aircraft returned to base without further incident. No capsule of nuclear materials was aboard the B-47 or installed in the weapon.

CDI: Accounts of this widely reported accident describe the bomb falling in the garden of the home of Mr. Walter Gregg in Mars Bluff, S.C. The high explosive detonation virtually destroyed his house creating a crater 50-70 feet in diameter and 25-30 feet deep. It caused minor injuries to Mr. Gregg and five members of his family, and additionally damaged five other houses and a church. The cleanup effort required several days. Air Force personnel recovered hundreds of pieces of bomb fragments that were carried off as souvenirs by local residents. The inhabitants of Mars Bluff were examined for several months to see if they had been exposed to any radiation. Five months later the Gregg family was awarded $54,000 from the Air Force. After this accident Air Force crews were ordered to "lock in" nuclear bombs. This reduced the possibility of accidental drops but increased the hazards if the plane crashed.

Triggering a Nuclear Exchange
The explosion of a nuclear device by accident — mechanical or human — could be a disaster for the United States, for its allies, and for its enemies. If one of these devices accidentally exploded, I would hope that both sides had sufficient means of verification and control to prevent the accident from triggering a nuclear exchange. But we cannot be certain that this would be the case.

John T. McNaughton
Assistant Secretary of Defense, 1962

No. 14, 4 November 1958 / B-47 / Dyess Air Force Base, [Abilene,] Texas

A B-47 caught fire on takeoff. Three crew members successfully ejected; one was killed when the aircraft crashed from an altitude of 1,500 feet. One nuclear weapon was on board when the aircraft crashed. The resultant detonation of the high explosive made a crater 35 feet in diameter and six feet deep. Nuclear materials were recovered near the crash site.

No. 15, 26 November 1958 / B-47 / Chennault Air Force Base, [Lake Charles,] Louisiana [now closed]

A B-47 caught fire on the ground. The single nuclear weapon on board was destroyed by the fire. Contamination was limited to the immediate vicinity of the weapon residue within the aircraft wreckage.

CDI: This is the eighth and last acknowledged B-47 accident, making it the most accident-prone of the nuclear-capable systems reported.

———— ⚭ ————

No. 16, 18 January 1959 / F-100 / Pacific base

The aircraft was parked on a reveted hardstand in ground alert configuration. The external load consisted of a weapon on the left intermediate station and three fuel tanks (both inboard stations and the right intermediate station). When the starter button was depressed during a practice alert, an explosion and fire occurred when the external fuel tanks inadvertently jettisoned. Fire trucks at the scene put out the fire in about seven minutes. The capsule was not in the vicinity of the aircraft and was not involved in the accident. There were no contamination or cleanup problems.

CDI: During the late 1950s and early 1960s the F-100 Super Sabre served as a primary interceptor. The F-100 could carry nuclear capable air-to-air missiles. In 1959 the United States had bases in the Pacific on Okinawa, in the Philippines, Taiwan, South Korea and Thailand. Two-thousand two-hundred ninety-four F-100s of all types were produced.

———— ⚭ ————

No. 17, 6 July 1959 / C-124 / Barksdale Air Force Base, [Bossier City,] Louisiana

A C-124 on a nuclear logistics movement mission crashed on takeoff. The aircraft was destroyed by fire which also destroyed one weapon. No nuclear or high explosive detonation occurred — safety devices functioned as designed. Limited contamination was present over a very small area immediately below the destroyed weapon. This contamination did not hamper rescue or fire fighting operations.

———— ⚭ ————

No. 18, 25 September 1959 / P-5M / Off Whidbey Island, Washington

A U.S. Navy P-5M aircraft ditched in Puget Sound off Whidbey Island, Washington. It was carrying an unarmed nuclear anti-submarine weapon containing no nuclear material. The weapon was not recovered.

CDI: The crew of ten was rescued. The prime mission of the P-5M was anti-submarine warfare. Weapons used for this purpose include nuclear depth charges which have an explosive power of five-ten kilotons (one kiloton equals 1,000 tons of TNT). The bomb dropped on Hiroshima has been estimated to have been 13.5 kilotons.

No. 19, 15 October 1959 / B-52/KC-135 / Hardinsberg, Kentucky

The B-52 departed Columbus Air Force Base, Mississippi, at 2:30 p.m. Central Standard Time, 15 October 1959. This aircraft assumed the #2 position in a flight of two. The KC-135 departed Columbus Air Force Base at 5:33 p.m. CST as the #2 tanker aircraft in a flight of two scheduled to refuel the B-52. Rendezvous for refueling was accomplished in the vicinity of Hardinsburg, Kentucky at 32,000 feet. It was night, weather was clear, and there was no turbulence. Shortly after the B-52 began refueling from the KC-135, the two aircraft collided. The instructor pilot and pilot of the B-52 ejected, followed by the electronic warfare officer and the radar navigator. The co-pilot, navigator, instructor navigator, and tail gunner failed to leave the B-52. All four crew members in the KC-135 were fatally injured. The B-52's two unarmed nuclear weapons were recovered intact. One had been partially burned but this did not result in the dispersion of any nuclear material or other contamination.

CDI: The B-52 entered service in June 1955 and continues to be the primary aircraft for the strategic bomber force. In 1959, the United States reached peak bomber strength of 1,366 B-47s and 488 B-52s. In the early 1960s, as much as 15% of the B-52 force (50-70 planes) was placed on airborne alert, in the air at all times armed and ready for attack. At that time B-52s carried from one to four nuclear bombs with yields between four and 24 megatons (one megaton equals 1,000,000 tons TNT). The present strategic bomber force includes 316 B-52s and 60 FB-111s.

No. 20, 7 June 1960 / BOMARC / McGuire Air Force Base, [near Trenton,] New Jersey

A BOMARC air defense missile in ready storage condition (permitting launch in two minutes) was destroyed by explosion and fire after a high pressure helium tank exploded and ruptured the missile's fuel tanks. The warhead was also destroyed by the fire although the high explosive did not detonate. Nuclear safety devices acted as designed. Contamination was restricted to an area immediately beneath the weapon and an adjacent elongated area approximately 100 feet long, caused by drain-off of fire fighting water.

CDI: The BOMARC missile was one of 56 housed at the 46th Air Defense Missile Squadron in Jackson Township, N.J., ten miles east of McGuire Air Force Base. Each missile was housed in a separate concrete and steel shelter. The BOMARC had earned a reputation as a dangerous weapon system. The *New York Times* reported the 47-foot missile "melted under an intense blaze fed by its 100-pound detonator of TNT . . . The atomic warhead apparently dropped into the molten mass that was left of the missile, which burned for forty-five minutes." The radiation "had been caused when thoriated magnesium metal which forms part the weapon, caught fire . . . the metal, already radioactive, becomes highly radioactive when it is burned."

No. 21, 24 January 1961 / B-52 / Goldsboro, North Carolina

During a B-52 airborne alert mission structural failure of the right wing resulted in two weapons separating from the aircraft during aircraft breakup at 2,000-10,000 feet altitude. One bomb parachute deployed and the weapon received little impact damage. The other bomb fell free and broke apart upon impact. No explosion occurred. Five of the eight crew members survived. A portion of one weapon, containing uranium, could not be recovered despite excavation in the waterlogged farmland to a depth of 50 feet. The Air Force subsequently purchased an easement requiring permission for anyone to dig there. There is no detectable radiation and no hazard in the area.

CDI: This report does not adequately convey the potential seriousness of the accident. The two weapons were 24 megaton nuclear bombs. Combined, they had the equivalent explosive power of 3,700 Hiroshima bombs. All of the bombs dropped on Japan and Germany in World War II totaled 2.2 megatons. The Office of Technology Assessment's study, *The Effects of Nuclear War,* calculated that a 25 megaton air burst on Detroit would result in 1.8 million fatalities and 1.3 million injuries. Upon recovering the intact bomb it was discovered, as Daniel Ellsberg has said, that "five of the six safety devices had failed." "Only a single switch," said nuclear physicist Ralph E. Lapp, "prevented the bomb from detonating and spreading fire and destruction over a wide area." This accident occurred four days after John F. Kennedy became President. He was told, according to *Newsweek,* that, "there had been more than 60 accidents involving nuclear weapons," since World War II, "including two cases in which nuclear-tipped anti-aircraft missiles were actually launched by inadvertence." As a result of the Goldsboro accident many new safety devices were placed on U.S. nuclear weapons and the Soviets were encouraged to do the same.

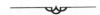

No. 22, 14 March 1961 / B-52 / Yuba City, California

A B-52 [from Mather Air Force Base near Sacramento] experienced failure of the crew compartment pressurization system forcing descent to 10,000 feet altitude. Increased fuel consumption caused fuel exhaustion before rendezvous with a tanker aircraft. The crew bailed out at 10,000 feet except for the aircraft commander who stayed with the aircraft to 4,000 feet, steering the plane away from a populated area. The two nuclear weapons on board were torn from the aircraft on ground impact. The high explosive did not detonate. Safety devices worked as designed and there was no nuclear contamination.

CDI: The crew of eight survived though a fireman died extinguishing the fire. The nuclear weapons involved could have been either the free fall bombs located in the interior bomb bay compartment or "Hound Dog" (AGM-28B) air-to-ground missiles which are carried in pairs beneath the wings of B-52s. The Hound Dog was a stand-off nuclear-tipped strategic missile with a range of 500-600 miles. It was inertially guided and powered by a turbojet, air-breathing engine and had a warhead of about one megaton. It was first assigned to SAC in late 1959, and was part of the Air Force's nuclear inventory until it was phased out in 1977.

By July 1961, SAC had increased the percentage of the bomber force on 15-minute ground alert from approximately 33% to 50%.

Nothing Infallible

Some day there will be an accidental explosion of a nuclear weapon, a pure accident, which has nothing whatsoever to do with political plans, intentions, or operations. The human mind cannot construct something that is infallible. Accordingly, the laws of probability virtually guarantee such an accident — not because the United States is relaxing any of the conscientious precautions designed to prevent one, or because the Soviet Union is necessarily getting more careless with warheads, but simply because sheer numbers of weapons are increasing . . . Nuclear weapons will surely spread throughout the world. They may become available in international trade: even that is not to be excluded. With thousands of nuclear weapons in existence, the danger of a nuclear accident in the world is unquestionably increasing.

Oskar Morgenstern
The Question of National Defense

No. 23, 13 November 1963 / Atomic Energy Commission storage igloo / Medina Base, [San Antonio,] Texas

An explosion involving 123,000 lbs. of high explosive components of nuclear weapons caused minor injuries to three Atomic Energy Commission employees. There was little contamination from the nuclear components stored elsewhere in the building. The components were from obsolete weapons being disassembled.

CDI: While three employees were dismantling the high-explosive component of a nuclear bomb it began burning spontaneously, setting off the larger amount of high explosives. Three other accounts of incidents (as well as this one) involving components of nuclear weapons were supplied to Dr. Joel Larus of New York University by the AEC on 12 January 1966:

Hamburg, New York (4 January 1958): An eastbound Nickel Plate railroad freight train was derailed, and five cars carrying "AEC classified material" were involved in the accident. According to the report there was no damage to the material and no injury to AEC personnel escorting the shipment.

Winslow, Arizona (4 November 1961): A trailer truck caught
fire while carrying a small amount of radioactive material.
There was no contamination resulting from the fire.

Marietta, Georgia (3 December 1962): A Louisville and Nash-
ville train was derailed while carrying nuclear weapons components. The material was not damaged but three couriers
were injured.

Accidents of this sort probably happen more frequently than reported.
In December 1980 a Department of Energy trailer carrying plutonium
overturned on icy roads on Interstate 25 near Fort Collins, Colorado, on its
way from Richland, Washington, to Los Alamos, New Mexico. Each year
hundreds of nuclear convoys travel millions of miles on U.S. highways.
Even when there is no accident, exposure over a period of years to radioactive material by certain Department of Energy couriers and privately con-
tracted transporters and personnel may be carcinogenic. It has been estimated that nearly 120,000 persons have access to U.S. nuclear weapons
and weapons-grade fissionable material. A study on the hazards of low
level, intrinsic radiation inherent in nuclear weapons is being conducted
by the Defense Nuclear Agency and will be released in 1982.

The weapons work at Medina was phased out in 1966 and consolidated
with production activities in the Pantex, Texas (near Amarillo), and Bur-
lington, Iowa, final assembly plants.

No. 24, 13 January 1964 / B-52 / Cumberland, Maryland

A B-52D was en route from Westover Air Force Base, [Chicopee Falls,]
Massachusetts, to its home base at Turner Air Force Base, [Albany,] Georgia. The crash occurred approximately 17 miles SW of Cumberland,
Maryland. The aircraft was carrying two weapons. Both weapons were in
a tactical ferry configuration (no mechanical or electrical connections had
been made to the aircraft and the safing switches were in the "SAFE" position). Prior to the crash, the pilot had requested a change of altitude
because of severe air turbulence at 29,500 feet. The aircraft was cleared to
climb to 33,000 feet. During the climb, the aircraft encountered violent air
turbulence and aircraft structural failure subsequently occurred. Of the five
aircrew members, only the pilot and co-pilot survived. The gunner and

navigator ejected but died of exposure to sub-zero temperatures after successfully reaching the ground. The radar navigator did not eject and died upon aircraft impact. The crash site was an isolated mountainous and wooded area. The site had 14 inches of new snow covering the aircraft wreckage which was scattered over an area of approximately 100 yards square. The weather during the recovery and cleanup operation involved extreme cold and gusty winds. Both weapons remained in the aircraft until it crashed and were relatively intact in the approximate center of the wreckage area.

No. 25, 5 December 1964 / LGM 30B (Minuteman ICBM) / Ellsworth Air Force Base, [Rapid City,] South Dakota

The LGM 30B Minuteman I missile was on strategic alert at Launch Facility (LF) L-02, Ellsworth Air Force Base, South Dakota. Two airmen were dispatched to the LF to repair the inner zone (IZ) security system. In the midst of their checkout of the IZ system, one retrorocket in the spacer below the Reentry Vehicle (RV) fired, causing the RV to fall about 75 feet to the floor of the silo. When the RV struck the bottom of the silo, the arming and fusing/altitude control subsystem containing the batteries was torn loose, thus removing all source of power from the RV. The RV structure received considerable damage. All safety devices operated properly in that they did not sense the proper sequence of events to allow arming the warhead. There was no detonation or radioactive contamination.

CDI: The Minuteman I was a three stage intercontinental ballistic missile carrying a one megaton warhead. The first missiles became operational in November 1962. Throughout the 1960s and 1970s they were gradually replaced by Minutemen IIs and IIIs. The Office of Technology Assessment study calculated that a one megaton surface burst in Detroit would cause 70 square miles of property destruction, a quarter of a million fatalities, and half a million injuries.

No. 26, 8 December 1964 / B-58 / Bunker Hill (now Grissom) Air Force Base, [Peru,] Indiana

SAC aircraft were taxiing during an exercise alert. As one B-58 reached a position directly behind the aircraft on the runway ahead of it, the aircraft ahead brought advanced power. As a result of the combination of the jet blast from the aircraft ahead, the icy runway surface conditions, and the power applied to the aircraft while attempting to turn onto the runway, control was lost and the aircraft slid off the left hand side of the taxiway. The left main landing gear passed over a flush mounted taxiway light fixture and ten feet further along in its travel, grazed the left edge of concrete light base. Ten feet further, the left main landing gear struck a concrete electrical manhole box, and the aircraft caught on fire. When the aircraft came to rest, all three crew members aboard began abandoning the aircraft. The aircraft commander and defensive systems operator egressed with only minor injuries. The navigator ejected in his escape capsule, which impacted 548 feet from the aircraft. He did not survive. Portions of the five nuclear weapons on board burned; contamination was limited to the immediate area of the crash and was subsequently removed.

CDI: The B-58 supersonic bomber was operational from 1960-69 and 104 were built.

No. 27, 11 October 1965 / C-124 / Wright-Patterson Air Force Base, [near Dayton,] Ohio

The aircraft was being refueled in preparation for a routine logistics mission when a fire occurred at the aft end of the refueling trailer. The fuselage of the aircraft, containing only components of nuclear weapons and a dummy training unit, was destroyed by the fire. There were no casualties. The resultant radiation hazard was minimal. Minor contamination was found on the aircraft, cargo, and clothing of explosive ordnance disposal and fire fighting personnel, and was removed by normal cleaning.

No. 28, 5 December 1965 / A-4 / At sea, Pacific

An A-4 aircraft loaded with one nuclear weapon rolled off the elevator of a U.S. aircraft carrier and fell into the sea. The pilot, aircraft, and weapon were lost. The incident occurred more than 500 miles from land.

CDI: The A-4 is a lightweight attack bomber. The weapon may have been a B-43 nuclear bomb.

—— ∞ ——

No. 29, 17 January 1966 / B-52/KC-135 / Palomares, Spain

The B-52 and the KC-135 collided during a routine high altitude air refueling operation. Both aircraft crashed near Palomares, Spain. Four of the 11 crew members survived. The B-52 carried four nuclear weapons. One was recovered on the ground, and one was recovered from the sea, on 7 April after extensive search and recovery efforts. Two of the weapons' high explosive materials exploded on impact with the ground, releasing some radioactive materials. Approximately 1,400 tons of slightly contaminated soil and vegetation were removed to the United States for storage at an approved site. Representatives of the Spanish government monitored the cleanup operation.

CDI: The DoD summary is a typically low-key account of the most well-publicized nuclear accident which resulted in what has been described as "the most expensive, intensive, harrowing and feverish underwater search for a man-made object in world history." The B-52 was returning to Seymour Johnson Air Force Base at Goldsboro, North Carolina, after flying the southern route of the SAC air alert missions (codenamed "Chrome Dome"). It was attempting its third refueling of the mission with a KC-135 tanker from the American base at Moron, in southwestern Spain, near Sevilla. Although the official report of the cause of the accident was not released to the public, it is believed that while attempting to dock at 30,000 feet above the Spanish coast, the nozzle of the tanker's boom, which was supposed to hook up with the B-52's orifice, struck the bomber, ripping open the B-52 along its spine and causing aerodynamic stress which snapped the bomber into pieces. Flames spurted through both planes and the KC-135's 40,000 gallons of jet fuel ignited, killing its four crew members almost immediately. Four of the seven crew members of the B-52 managed to eject and parachute to safety.

As the two planes, worth $11,000,000 and weighing loaded nearly 800,000 lbs., crashed and burned, wreckage fell across an area of land and water of about 100 square miles. Of the four H-bombs (believed to be in the 20-25 megaton range) aboard, one fell to earth and remained relatively intact, two scattered plutonium widely over the fields of Palomares when their high explosive material detonated, and one fell into the ocean. For the next three months the village was turned upside down as the search, decontamination and removal operation began. Estimates for the amount of radioactive soil and vegetation removed to the nuclear dumping site at Aiken, South Carolina, range up to 1,750 tons.

The weapon that sank in the Mediterranean caused the greatest problem. Its recovery required the assembly of a naval task force, including a small armada of miniature research submarines, scuba teams, sonar experts, nuclear weapons engineers, oceanic photographers, and hundreds of sailors aboard ships of the Sixth Fleet which were called in to search the area. It took two weeks for the midget sub *Alvin* to sight the bomb, entangled in its parachute 12 miles off Palomares on a 70 degree slope at a depth of 2,500 feet. After a series of failed attempts, the bomb was finally recovered on 7 April, dented but intact, with no known radiation leakage. The Palomares search took about 80 days and required the services of 3,000 Navy personnel and 33 Navy vessels, not counting ships, planes and people used to move equipment to the site. By 1969, a U.S. commission had settled 522 claims by Palomares residents totaling $600,000. It also gave the town of Palomares the gift of a desalting plant, which cost about $200,000 to build.

Accidental Nuclear War
Despite the most elaborate precautions, it is conceivable that technical malfunction or human failure, a misinterpreted incident or unauthorized action, could trigger a nuclear disaster or nuclear war.

Introduction of U.S.-Soviet Treaty
U.S. Arms Control and Disarmament Agency, September 1971

No. 30, 21 January 1968 / B-52 / Thule, Greenland

A B-52 from Plattsburgh Air Force Base, New York, crashed and burned some seven miles southwest of the runway at Thule Air Base, Greenland, while approaching the base to land. Six of the seven crew members survived. The bomber carried four nuclear weapons, all of which were destroyed by fire. Some radioactive contamination occurred in the area of the crash, which was on the sea ice. Some 237,000 cubic feet of contaminated ice, snow and water, with crash debris, were removed to an approved storage site in the United States over the course of a four-month operation. Although an unknown amount of contamination was dispersed by the crash, environmental sampling showed normal readings in the area after the cleanup was completed. Representatives of the Danish government monitored the cleanup operation.

CDI: The B-52 was flying the Arctic Circle route as part of the continuous airborne alert operation, "Chrome Dome," involving anywhere from 6 to 50 B-52s. A fire broke out in the navigator's compartment and was soon out of control, spreading smoke throughout the plane. The pilot headed the bomber towards Thule Air Base, located about 700 miles above the Arctic Circle on the northwestern Greenland coast, to attempt an emergency landing. The seven crew members had to eject when the plane was at about 8-9,000 feet and about four miles south of the runway. Six of the crew members parachuted to safety with only slight injuries while one, the co-pilot, died. After it was abandoned, the plane did a 180 degree turn and crashed onto the ice of North Star Bay seven and one-half miles southwest of Thule, whereupon it skidded across the ice in flames and exploded. It is believed that the high explosives in the outer coverings of the four 1.1 megaton H-bombs aboard detonated, releasing radiation from the plutonium in the bombs and causing fires which destroyed all four. Wreckage of the plane was widely scattered in an area about 300 yards on either side of the plane's path, much of it in "cigarette box-sized" pieces. A team of 70 Air Force and civilian specialists were flown in to monitor radiation and search for debris and the bombs, soon followed by the Navy's special team which had worked at Palomares. The bombs' parts were discovered about ten days later on the snow within 1,000 feet of the path of the plane.

A massive collection and removal effort began. The contaminated ice and crash debris were removed to the United States, the bomb debris to the AEC Pantex plant at Amarillo, Texas, where the bombs had been manufactured. A few days after the crash, Secretary of Defense McNamara ordered the removal of nuclear weapons from planes on airborne alert. The alerts were later curtailed and then suspended altogether.

The government of Denmark, which owns Greenland and prohibits nuclear weapons on or over their territory, issued a strong protest. There were large demonstrations throughout Denmark against the U.S. and its base at Thule. Costs of the crash, cleanup and compensation ran into the millions of dollars.

⌇⌇

No. 31, Spring 1968 / At sea, Atlantic, details remain classified

CDI: The accident probably refers to the nuclear powered attack submarine USS *Scorpion*. The *Scorpion* was last heard from on 21 May 1968. It was returning to Norfolk, Va., after a three-month training exercise with the Sixth Fleet in the Mediterranean. It sank 400-450 miles southwest of the Azores. Initial suspicion that the Soviets were somehow involved was allayed when the research ship *Mizar* photographed the wreckage at 10,000 feet on the sea floor. A Navy seven-man court of inquiry met for 11 weeks and heard 90 witnesses. They found "no evidence of any kind to suggest foul play or sabotage," and that the "certain cause of the *Scorpion* cannot be ascertained from evidence available." Ninety-nine men were lost. The nuclear weapons aboard may have been either SUBROC or ASTOR, or both. SUBROC, first deployed in 1965, is an anti-submarine missile and nuclear depth charge. Attack submarines normally carry four-six SUBROCs, which have a range of 25-30 miles and high explosive power. ASTOR is the nuclear version of the MK45 torpedo which went into service around 1960 and has low explosive power.

⌇⌇

No. 32, 19 September 1980 / Titan II ICBM / Damascus, Arkansas

During routine maintenance in a Titan II silo, Air Force repairman dropped a heavy wrench socket, which rolled off a work platform and toward the bottom of the silo. The socket bounced and struck the missile, causing a leak from a pressurized fuel tank. The missile complex and the surrounding area were evacuated and a team of specialists was called in from Little Rock Air Force Base, the missile's main support base. About eight and a half hours after the initial puncture, fuel vapors within the silo ignited and exploded. The explosion fatally injured one member of the team. Twenty-one other U.S. AF personnel were injured. The missile's reentry vehicle, which contained a nuclear warhead was recovered intact. There was no radioactive contamination.

CDI: The explosion of the volatile fuel blew off the 740 ton silo door of reinforced concrete and steel and catapulted the warhead 600 feet. The 54 liquid-fueled Titan II missiles have been operational since 1963. It is estimated that Titan II ICBMs carry a 9 megaton warhead. The Office of

Technology Assessment estimated that a 9 megaton airburst on Leningrad would result in 2.4 million fatalities and 1.1 million injuries. With age, the seals on the missiles are corroding, increasing the number of leaks. The worst missile accident occurred in Searcy, Arkansas, on 9 August 1965, when a fire in a Titan II silo killed 53. The Air Force has disclosed that between 1975 and 1979 there have been 125 accidents at Titan sites in Arkansas, Arizona, and Kansas. From March 1979 to September 1980 there were ten other leaks and accidents at Arkansas Titan sites. On 24 August 1978, at a Titan site in Rock, Kansas, two airmen were killed and 30 others injured when they were exposed to deadly oxidizer gas. The silo at Damascus, Arkansas, will be filled in gravel while that at Rock, Kansas, is being refurbished and is planned to be operational in September 1982.

CDI Conclusions

- The Department of Defense report on nuclear weapons accidents is a clear warning of the continuing danger of nuclear accidents.
- The variety of nuclear weapons accidents which have occurred in the past and the increased numbers of nuclear weapons suggest that more accidents and perhaps more serious accidents will occur in the future.
- A General Accounting Office or other governmental organization investigation is needed to identify major risks and preventive measures in order to reduce the possibility of accidents in the future.
- Development and promulgation of U.S. government plans for handling emergencies arising from nuclear weapons accidents could reduce civilian casualties in areas where nuclear weapons are stored or handled.

Author's Comments

In general, the Center for Defense Information comments on the brief Department of Defense accounts of the 32 incidents provided additional relevant information. However, a few of the CDI comments are in error:

1. The Minuteman I missile is not BOMARC (Boeing ground-to-air missile), as indicated in the Introduction.

2. No. 7 indicated that the Mark 6 had about 8,000 pounds of TNT as part of its trigger mechanism. The total weight of the Mark 6 was 7,600 pounds. The weight of the bomb case, fusing and firing components, nuclear materials, etc., was a considerable percentage of the total weight; hence, the high explosive weighed considerably less than 8,000 pounds. In addition, the Mark 6 was 60 inches in diameter (rather than 72 inches) and 128 inches long (rather than 144 inches).
3. No. 21 indicated that the yield of the bombs in this accident was 24 megatons; the yield was in the megaton range.
4. No. 29 indicated that the missing B28 was found at sea 12 miles off Palomares; the correct distance was about five miles.

The 1981 CDI Conclusions (which included recommendations) were very strong and suggested that the Government Accounting Office or other government agencies needed to identify major risks and preventive measures. The DoD and the AEC/DOE took strong preventive safety measures after the Palomares and Thule accidents of 1966 and 1968. As a result, there have been no nuclear weapon accidents (to the best of my knowledge) since the Titan II accident of September 1980.

Appendix B

Letters of
Commendation

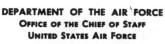

DEPARTMENT OF THE AIR FORCE
OFFICE OF THE CHIEF OF STAFF
UNITED STATES AIR FORCE
WASHINGTON, D.C.

GAF
8096/7
CE

		Code
FOWLER	~	
SHUSTER		
POPE		2
SCRIVNER		
McKNIGHT		
FILE		
DESTROY		
RETURN		

3 1 MAY 1966

cy to 1000
6/8

Mr. S. P. Schwartz, President
Sandia Corporation
P.O. Box 5800
Albuquerque, New Mexico

Dear Mr. Schwartz

The Sandia Corporation representatives who responded to the recent
accident near Palomares, Spain, provided invaluable assistance to
the United States Air Force. Your representative, Mr. Stuart V.
Asselin, a member of the initial team from the Albuquerque area and
a participant in the final phases of the operation, was especially
helpful. Dedication and educated performance contributed significantly
in locating, identifying, and properly disposing of the nuclear weapons
involved.

Other Sandia Corporation personnel who assisted during the operations
were Mr. S. A. Moore, Mr. R. C. Maydew, Mr. W. R. Barton, Mr. W. R.
Hoagland, and Mr. R. E. Reed. They formed the best team that could
have been provided for the task to be performed.

I sincerely appreciate the efforts of Mr. Asselin and all the others
in successfully carrying out a sensitive, difficult operation in a
professional and cooperative manner.

Sincerely

HEWITT T. WHELESS, Lt General, USAF
Assistant Vice Chief of Staff

DEPARTMENT OF THE AIR FORCE
HEADQUARTERS STRATEGIC AIR COMMAND
OFFUTT AIR FORCE BASE, NEBRASKA, 68113

a h o o - Director of
Storage Operations

2 MAR 1966

Mr. Walter White
~~United States~~ Atomic Energy Commission
Albuquerque, New Mexico

Dear Mr. White

Please extend my personal thanks to Mr. Randall C. Maydew, Sandia
Corporation, for his invaluable assistance to the Strategic Air Command and the United States Air Force during the Broken Arrow operation
at Palomares, Spain.

The technical skill and professional knowledge that Mr. Maydew provided
was most outstanding and reflects great credit upon him as well as upon
your organization.

JOHN D. RYAN, General, USAF   1 Atch
Commander in Chief   Ltr 16AF, 16 Feb 1966.

Mighty fine!

	Code
FOWLER	2
SHUSTER	
POPE	2
SCRIVNER	
McKNIGHT	
FILE	
DESTROY	
RETURN	

MAR 9 1966

Rec'd by ORG. 1 MAR - 9 1966

Peace . . . . is our Profession

Very good! DC7 3-9-66

DEPARTMENT OF THE AIR FORCE
HEADQUARTERS SIXTEENTH AIR FORCE (SAC)
APO NEW YORK 09283

REPLY TO
ATTN OF: C

16 February 1966

SUBJECT: Appreciation

TO: General John D. Ryan, USAF
       Commander in Chief
       Strategic Air Command
       Offutt Air Force Base, Nebraska 68113

       Mr. Walter White
       United States Atomic Energy Commission
       Albuquerque, New Mexico

IN TURN

1.   From 29 January to 8 February 1966, Mr. Randall C.
Maydew, Sandia Corporation, performed invaluable service
during search and rescue operations at Palomares, Spain.
Flying in from the United States on extremely short notice,
he joined with other specialists in the search area to form
my Systems Analysis Team. Working together, these highly
competent individuals obtained a briefing on the accident and
immediately set about gathering facts, reviewing the Aircraft
Accident Board testimony, conducting interviews of special
witnesses, and forwarding data gathered on the scene to
agencies in the United States for machine computation and
analysis.

2.   Having unselfishly spent long hours under adverse field
conditions, the team submitted to me a detailed and comprehensive theoretical study that forms the basis for further
search operations. Moreover, team members provided Rear
Admiral Guest, Task Force 65 Commander, me, and our
staffs, very enlightening briefings governing our daily search
activities.

3.   I commend Mr. Maydew and wish to express my deep
appreciation for his assistance. My thanks also to the
Sandia Corporation for a rapid and productive response to
all requests.

DELMAR E. WILSON
Major General, USAF
Commander

Peace . . . . is our Profession

Notes

Prologue

1. "The Palomares Accident — An Interview with Randall C. Maydew," conducted by Mecah S. Furman, Nuclear Safety Oral History Series, 40-minute video produced by Sandia National Laboratories Nuclear Safety Information Center for the Weapons Emergency Management Division of the Albuquerque Field Office of the Department of Energy, December 1991; "Vital Contributions Made by Sandia in Locating Lost Nuclear Weapon," *Lab News,* Sandia Corporation, 22 April 1966, Sandia Corporate Archives; "The Young Man and the Bomb in the Sea," *Lab News,* Sandia National Laboratories, 11 April 1986, Sandia Corporate Archives.

2. Howard held this Pentagon position from 1963 to 1966; he returned to Sandia in 1966 as vice president responsible for nuclear weapon development and later became the executive vice president. During this era, the development and production of nuclear weapons proceeded at a very rapid pace, which required close coordination between the AEC and the DoD.

3. Sandia was operated by the University of California from 1945-1949 and by AT&T from 1949-1993. Lockheed Martin Corporation currently operates Sandia.

4. Los Alamos Scientific Laboratory, now Los Alamos National Laboratory, was formed in 1943 as part of the Army Manhattan Engineer District to do the research, development, design, and testing of nuclear warheads for bombs, shells, and missiles. They have been operated by the University of California, Berkeley, since 1943. Lawrence Livermore National Laboratory, Livermore, California (also operated by the University of California), was formed in 1952 to provide a redundant (to Los Alamos) nuclear warhead design capability.

5. I retired from Sandia in 1991 and then helped produce a video, "The Palomares Accident — An Interview with Randall C. Maydew," to document the Palomares incident for the nuclear safety groups at Sandia and the DOE (see Sandia Corporate Archives). That video was the genesis of this book.

6. Commander W. M. Place, Colonel F. C. Cobb, and Lieutenant Colonel C. G. Deffeding, "Palomares Summary Report," Field Command, Defense Nuclear Agency (DNA), Technology and Analysis, Kirtland Air Force Base, NM, 15 January 1975, 216 pp. (see p. 75).

This document, with 17 references, is an excellent summary of the Air Force, Navy, and Army documentation of the Palomares accident. Only 25 copies were printed and distributed.

7. A detailed listing, with discussion, of the 32 United States nuclear accidents that occurred from 1950 to 1980 (no known accidents have occurred since 1980) is given in Appendix A. This historical review puts the Palomares accident into perspective.

Chapter 1

8. Some information in this chapter comes from Flora Lewis, *One of Our H-Bombs is Missing* (New York: McGraw-Hill Book Company, 1967), 270 pp. (see p. 4). Lewis, a respected reporter with extensive publications, carefully researched the subject and conducted many interviews with the participants. Her book provides accurate information on the refueling accident, the search, and the recovery. She interviewed me in Albuquerque in the spring of 1966. One small error in her book is on page 158; W. R. Barton, rather than I, interviewed the pharmacist and his assistant about their sighting of the #4 H-bomb entering the sea. See also Colonel George N. Payne, Accident Board President, 16th Air Force, Torrejon Air Base, Spain, "USAF Accident/Incident Report," 31 January 1966, 172 pp.; a copy of this unclassified report was furnished to me in July 1994 by Colonel John R. Clapper, Commander, Headquarters Air Force Safety Agency, Department of the Air Force, Kirtland AFB, New Mexico. See also Place, Cobb, and Deffeding, 13.

9. Tad Szulc, *The Bombs of Palomares* (New York: Viking Press, 1967), 274 pp. (see p. 22). Szulc was the Madrid Bureau Chief of *The New York Times* at the time of the Palomares accident. He carefully researched the subject and conducted many interviews with the participants. His book provides accurate information of the Palomares incident. One error is the weight of the B28 bomb: he indicated (on p. 17) the weight was 5,000 pounds; the correct weight was 2,250 pounds.

10. Szulc, 28.

11. Zulu time is the same as Greenwich time. It is a military designation for a zero reference.

12. See Payne.
13. Place, Cobb, and Deffeding, 13, 16.
14. Place, Cobb, and Deffeding, 13.
15. Lewis, 61.
16. Place, Cobb, and Deffeding, 17.
17. Place, Cobb, and Deffeding, 183. See also Lewis, 167; Szulc, 214; and
    Christopher Morris, *The Day They Lost the H-Bomb* (New York: Cow-
    ard-McCann, Inc., 1966), 192 pp. (see pp. 46, 104, 120, 140, 162, and
    173). Morris was a British correspondent in Spain for *The London
    Daily Express* at the time of the Palomares incident. His book is well
    researched and provides the most complete documentation of the reac-
    tion of the world press to the Palomares nuclear accident.
18. Place, Cobb, and Deffeding, 183.

Chapter 2

19. Place, Cobb, and Deffeding, 20.
20. Lewis, 17; Szulc, 7; Place, Cobb, and Deffeding, 19.
21. Randall C. Maydew and Carl W. Peterson, *Design and Testing of High
    Performance Parachutes,* AGARDograph 319 (Essex, England: Advi-
    sory Group for Aerospace Research and Development, NATO, 1991),
    300 pp.
22. Place, Cobb, and Deffeding, 48.
23. Place, Cobb, and Deffeding, 185.
24. Place, Cobb, and Deffeding, 185.
25. Place, Cobb, and Deffeding, 185.
26. Place, Cobb, and Deffeding, 185.

Chapter 3

27. "Searching for the Bomb at Palomares," Recollections for Tomorrow,
    1949-1989, in Observance of the 40th Anniversary of Sandia Nation-
    al Laboratories, p. 18, Sandia Public Relations and Technical Com-
    munications Department, November 1989, Sandia Corporate Archives;
    see *Lab News* articles in note 1 above; see also Sandia National Labo-
    ratories technical files on Palomares.

28. Place, Cobb, and Deffeding, 76-78.
29. Place, Cobb, and Deffeding, 187.
30. Place, Cobb, and Deffeding, 187.

Chapter 4

31. Message from Directorate, Nuclear Safety, Kirtland AFB, New Mexico, to 16th AF, Torrejon AB, Spain, dated 28 January 1966:

   In response to General Wilson's request for assistance on the scene, Mr. Randall C. Maydew, Q clearance (Secret) granted 22 Apr 52, file #5603-AB, DOB 29 Jan 24, from Sandia Corp., will arrive Madrid on TWA flight 900, 1100 hrs Madrid time, 29 Jan Request Mr. Maydew be met at Madrid for expeditious transportation to Gen Wilson's command post.

32. Lewis, 80.
33. Memo from R. C. Maydew and W. R. Barton through A. Y. Pope to G. A. Fowler, Vice President, Sandia Corporation, "Chronological Summary of Significant Events in the Participation in Broken Arrow Operation," 29 March 1966, Sandia Corporate Archives. See also Place, Cobb, and Deffeding, 84; Lewis, 148, 155; Szulc, 35, 183; and Morris, 21, 62.
34. Memo from R. C. Maydew and W. R. Barton to G. A. Fowler, Sandia Corporate Archives.
35. Place, Cobb, and Deffeding, 189.
36. Place, Cobb, and Deffeding, 203.
37. Place, Cobb, and Deffeding, 189-90.
38. Place, Cobb, and Deffeding, 192.

Chapter 5

39. Dr. Langham discussed the Palomares accident in a 1968 paper, "The Problem of Large-Area Plutonium Contamination" (presented at and published by Bureau of Radiological Health Seminar Program, Maryland, 6 December 1968), U.S. Department of Health, Education, and Welfare, PB-184020.

40. Place, Cobb, and Deffeding, 63.
41. Place, Cobb, and Deffeding, 53, 54.
42. Place, Cobb, and Deffeding, 54-55.
43. Place, Cobb, and Deffeding, 55.
44. Place, Cobb, and Deffeding, 66.
45. Place, Cobb, and Deffeding, 181.

Chapter 6
46. Commander (Ret.) Everett S. Allen, "Research Submarine Alvin," U.S. Naval Institute Proceedings, April 1964.
47. Lewis, 204.
48. Place, Cobb, and Deffeding, 193.
49. Place, Cobb, and Deffeding, 194.
50. Szulc, 242.
51. Place, Cobb, and Deffeding, 194.
52. Place, Cobb, and Deffeding, 203.
53. *Dictionary of American Naval Fighting Ships,* Vol. 5 (Washington, D.C.: Naval History Division, USN Department, 1970).
54. Place, Cobb, and Deffeding, 200.

Epilogue
55. "How They Found the Bomb," *Time,* 13 May 1966.
56. Szulc, 138; Lewis, 240; and Morris, 57.
57. Scott D. Sagan, *The Limits of Safety, Organizations, Accidents, and Nuclear Weapons,* Princeton Studies in International History and Politics (Princeton: Princeton University Press, 1993), 178.
58. Sagan, 51.
59. Sagan, 51.
60. Sagan, 51.
61. Herman Mauney, interview by author, 21 August 1994, National Atomic Museum, Albuquerque. Mauney started his career as a weapon designer at Sandia in 1953. He worked closely with Los Alamos National Laboratory personnel in weaponizing their warhead designs. He became one of Sandia's principals in nuclear safety and weapons

evaluation. He was promoted to ever-increasing management responsibilities until his retirement as Director of Systems Evaluation in 1991.

62. Major R. W. Simmons, USMC, "Broken Arrow," Surety Information Letter No. 93-01, 1993, Interservice Nuclear Weapons School, Kirtland AFB, Albuquerque, NM.

63. Edward Schumacher, "Where H-Bombs Fell, Spaniards Still Worry," *The New York Times,* 28 December 1985.

⚓

Appendix A

64. Chief of Naval Operations, U.S. Department of the Navy, 15 July 1978.

⚓

Suggested Reading

Furman, Mecah Stewart. *Sandia National Laboratory: The Postwar Decade*. Albuquerque: University of New Mexico Press, 1989.

Gosling, F. G. "The Manhattan Project: Making the Atomic Bomb." DOE/HR-0096, September 1994. Available from Office of Scientific and Technical Information, Oak Ridge, TN.

Johnson, Leland. *Oak Ridge National Laboratory: The First 50 Years*. Knoxville: University of Tennessee Press, 1994.

Kevles, Daniel. *The Physicists*. Cambridge, MA: Harvard University Press, 1987.

Rhodes, Richard. *The Making of the Atomic Bomb*. New York: Simon and Schuster, 1988.

Index

by Lori L. Daniel